ORSER
A SKATER'S LIFE

ORSER
A SKATER'S LIFE

BRIAN ORSER WITH STEVE MILTON

KEY PORTER BOOKS

Canadian Cataloguing in Publication Data

Orser, Brian, 1961–
  Orser : a skater's life

ISBN 1-55013-126-5

1. Orser, Brian, 1961–   . 2. Skaters — Canada —
Biography. 3. Skating — Canada — History.
I. Milton, Steve. II. Title.

GV850.O77A3   1988   796.91'092'4   C88-094339-4

Key Porter Books Limited
70 The Esplanade
Toronto, Ontario
M5E 1R2

The publisher gratefully acknowledges the assistance
of the Ontario Arts Council.

Design: Marie Bartholomew
Phototypesetting: Computer Composition of Canada, Inc.

Printed and bound in Canada by
T.H. Best Printing Company Limited

88 89 90 91 92   6 5 4 3 2 1

Contents

ORSER
A SKATER'S LIFE

Prologue

Just three weeks before the 1988 Winter Olympics, Butch Orser stood rinkside at the Toronto Cricket, Skating and Curling Club, his gaze fixed on a slender figure waiting alone at the other end of the ice.

Dressed in white turtleneck and black sweat pants, readying himself for an impromptu session of interpretive skating, was Butch's son Brian.

For months, Butch and Joanne Orser had anxiously watched their youngest child withstand what was arguably the most intense pressure ever exerted upon a single Canadian athlete. With the Olympics scheduled for his native country, he was Canada's only defending World champion in a Winter Olympic sport. He bore the collective hopes and expectations of an entire nation.

As the first strains of "Danse Macabre" issued from the rink's sound system, Brian stretched, seeming to grow taller than his five feet seven inches. Then, he began to skate.

Earlier, there had been other skaters on the practice ice, but now the small rink was deserted, leaving Brian Orser alone with his music. The Cricket Club is a place where protocol and a sense of occasion are readily understood. Donald Jackson and other legendary Canadian skaters had trained there and they, too, had been afforded time and space to skate on their own.

Moving smoothly backwards, Brian responded to the music with an intricate, unplanned series of skating maneuvers: he twisted and dipped through slower portions, sprinkled spins and triple jumps across faster sections, and rippled through dazzling footwork sequences as the tempo quickened and the music grew loud.

By the time he had finished, exhausted, nearly an hour later, a crowd of two dozen or more club members was pressed against the windows of the second-floor dining room, which overlooks the ice surface.

Butch Orser, still standing by the side of the rink, was in awe.

"I felt like he was the conductor and he was telling the music what to do," recalls Butch. "What he made you listen to was not the melody but the undercurrent, the part you always knew was there, but never really noticed before.

"When he finished, I asked him if it was for a new program and he said, 'No, I was just out there doing what I started skating for.' I was stunned. If I never see skating again, I've seen it all."

Butch Orser had seen what Brian Orser calls "the essence of skating" — a feeling uniting man, music, blades and ice that kept him on skates nearly every day for twenty years. As he matured, he grew more familiar with that essence, but it had been with him since he first set foot on the ice.

At 7:30 A.M., on December 18, 1961, Joanne Orser, then twenty-six, gave birth to her fifth and last child, a son, in the Belleville, Ontario, General Hospital. It was a routine delivery. Outside in the waiting room, her twenty-eight-year-old husband paced nervously. His given name was Harl, reflecting his Dutch heritage, but after age three, no one ever called him anything but Butch.

It was exactly one week before Christmas. The eldest children — five-year-old Janice, and Bob, who was four — were old enough to anticipate the approaching festivities, and their excitement had been heightened by the birth of their new brother and the seasonal cold and snowy weather the night before.

On another wintry night less than three months later — March 15, 1962 — four thousand miles from that burgeoning Belleville family, Canadian sporting history was made.

Twenty-two-year-old Donald Jackson from Oshawa, just a few minutes' travel from Belleville, captivated a crowd of eighteen thousand in Prague's Fucik Arena, to edge Czechoslovakian hero Karol Divin for the World figure-skating championship. It was the first time a Canadian man had won the title in the fifty-two-year history of the World championships (Canada had competed since 1928) and the win was crafted in spectacular fashion. After figures, Divin held a whopping forty-five-point lead. He skated ahead of the Canadian in the freeskating final, in front of a partisan crowd. But Jackson was a brilliant freeskater and successfully completed the first triple Lutz jump — thought so difficult at the time that not another was landed at the World level for a dozen years — and ran together a string of flashy moves to capture a total of seven perfect 6.0 marks, a record that stood until the mastery of ice dancers Torvill and Dean was acknowledged by judges more than twenty years later.

Jackson would turn professional after that championship, but his influence on Canadian skating would not end there. Like Barbara Ann Scott, who won women's World and Olympic titles for Canada in 1947 and 1948, he inspired a wave of youngsters to discover and stick with the sport. He was a guest skater in scores of local skating shows, bringing World-championship style and maneuvers to small clubs across the country. Gregarious, always smiling, and easily accessible, he is still sought-after by skating parents, coaches and media to offer his comments or encouragement.

As a youngster, Brian Orser would meet Donald Jackson at a local club show. The two men's careers were similar, though separated by two decades. Both were small-town Ontario boys who eventually became World champions. Each had a difficult trademark jump and forced a generation of skaters to radically upgrade their technical capabilities. Both men knew elation and heartbreak at the World level.

Jackson's performance in Prague is often referred to as the greatest singles performance of all time. With it were introduced some major themes that would be repeated in Canadian men's skating over the rest of the century. Canadians would regularly grapple with the compulsory figures; they would have to struggle to make up huge scoring gaps with dynamic, daring and innovative freeskating; they would have to overcome the psychological handicap of having to come from behind.

Jackson had already established another Canadian men's trademark: the near-miss. Before striking gold, he had finished fourth once; second, twice; and had been third in the Olympics.

Donald McPherson won the title in 1963 and it appeared briefly that these back-to-back successes were merely the visible surface of a bottomless well of future triumphs. But after McPherson, there were only two other Canadians who challenged for the World title. Toller Cranston was World freeskating champion in 1974 and 1975, but could never quite win the gold medal. Brian Orser finally did.

It was an arid twenty-four years after McPherson's trip to the podium and a quarter-century, less three days, after Jackson's brilliant freeskate, that Brian Orser became the third Canadian man ever to win the World championship.

1. A Small-town Boy

When I was four years old, my dad received the phone call that altered the course of our family's life.

On the other end of the line was a man named Ted Cuthbert from the Penetang Bottling Company, which bottled Coca-Cola. The business, which operated in Ontario's cottage country, was struggling. Ted wanted to know if my father would consider a job managing the firm.

My dad wasn't really interested. His career with Coca-Cola was progressing steadily. He was about to be made a sales manager, after years in sales and driving a delivery truck, but he decided to investigate the opportunity offered by this privately owned company.

At the meeting, Dad told the owners that he was interested in running the plant, but that he wanted to be able to purchase part of the business on a long-term basis through bonuses. They balked, but Dad stood his ground. Eventually they gave in, and the seven of us were on the way to Penetang.

Dad's strong stand was a turning point in my life — if anyone that young can have a turning point — because it took me north. There I would discover figure skating and meet Doug Leigh, who has remained my coach for nearly twenty years. And because my parents worked so hard at the bottling business, they were able to assemble the financial resources to buy the business and to cover the considerable expense of figure skating for my two sisters and me. It was a prime example of one of our family's strong traits: we remain firm on those things we believe in. That firmness — sometimes it's just plain stubbornness — is ingrained in all five of the Orser children.

Actually, we didn't move to Penetang, but to 411 Hugle Avenue in Midland, which is essentially its twin city, or twin *town*. Midland is larger than Penetang, but when you're talking about populations of around five thousand, you're talking small-town Ontario.

One thing I do recall about moving to the house on Hugle Avenue was that it was smaller than the Belleville house, which had four bedrooms. This place had only three. Since my parents had one room, and Janice and Mary Kay shared another, Bob, Mike and I — aged 8, 7 and 4 — were squeezed into the third. There were two bunk beds and I slept in a bottom berth until I was older and my mom felt confident enough to allow me up top.

Midland was, and still is, a small town. Winters are desolate and bitter. The whole area is often paralyzed by snow or ice storms that blow in off Georgian Bay. Summers, however, are bustling. Both Penetang and Midland are vacation towns. They serve as markets and harbors for the thousands of cottagers on the sandy mainland shores and rocky islands of Georgian Bay.

For kids interested in sports, as we all were, it was an

excellent place to grow up. Winters were so cold and snowy that there were always outdoor rinks and ponds to skate and play hockey on. And there was a ski hill, Mountainview, nearby. In the summer, we had access to boating and some of the best freshwater beaches in the world. My parents eventually bought a cottage on Georgian Bay, although by then, I was ten years old, and didn't have much time to enjoy it because I spent at least eight weeks of my summer at skating school.

Ours was a normal small-town childhood. Everybody in town knew everybody else. I was too young for school when we first moved there, but my brothers and sisters were all registered at the Catholic school, St. Mary's. I started there the next September.

That first winter in Midland, my mother took me to a preschool skating program at the old Midland Arena. My oldest sister, Janice, began skating in a club in Windsor when she was only two years old but, when they moved to Belleville, my parents found that the skating club there was too expensive. In Midland, Janice started taking lessons after school and on the weekends with the Midland Figure Skating Club, which leased ice time at the arena. When Mom took Janice to the lessons, she had to take Mary Kay and me along, too, because we were too young to leave at home alone. Since we were already at the rink, it was decided to plop us into group lessons. I still have that first pair of skates — white CCMs, which we spray-painted black.

Right from the start I loved skating, maybe because I mastered the basics quickly. I wanted to become good at it. Even then, it was important to me to be the best at whatever I did. I can't remember ever not feeling that way. For instance, when I was six or seven, I made a cup of tea for Janice, and she told me that I made the best tea in the family. I already looked up to my big sister and from that point on, I always made her tea.

My parents always got a kick out of the fact that everything

I wore to school in grades one and two had to match perfectly, even the underwear and socks. I was going to school and wanted to look the part of a student. And in those early years, I always wanted to skate the fastest, to be the one people watched. I'm a perfectionist. I don't get vicious, and I really don't like having to beat somebody to get to the top, but I want to get there.

I wasn't really coached too much. The club teachers were concerned strictly with recreational figure skating. They didn't know anything about jumps, or even the names of them, other than the very basic ones. I don't think there was anybody in the skating school doing jumps. I didn't see someone doing a perfect jump and say, "Hey, I want to do that." I have to try something myself before I decide if I like it. In Midland, I had no hero to imitate; I just started messing around on my own.

I hadn't the foggiest notion about technique. I just knew that I loved to go fast and that I loved to jump high. The speed and the sense of freedom were what attracted me to it. I fell in love with the sensation. The idea of sensation is a big thing in my life. I loved swimming and diving because of the sensation of floating and being surrounded by water. When I went to school, I gravitated toward tumbling and gymnastics.

In the living room of our house on Hugle Avenue we had a leather footstool with a springy, cushioned top. When I was seven, I would run full speed from one end of the living room to the other and do a headspring off that footstool. I did it for hours at a time, springing off my head, flipping through the air and landing on my feet. My parents would be in the basement, watching TV, and hear this BANG when I hit the footstool and another BANG when I hit the floor. My dad's friend Mart Forget used to come over and say, "Brian, spin for us." So I'd stand on my head on the stool and spin around — breakdancing a dozen years before its time — and everyone would break up laughing.

I loved the feeling of freedom produced by jumping, spinning, flipping or just being in midair. I can remember special moments from downhill skiing that gave me those sensations. At about the same period that I was crashing off the footstool, our whole family used to ski at Mountainview, which was close to our house. Sometimes I'd walk over with a friend of Janice's and spend the whole day there. There was this big knoll on one of the runs — to an eight-year-old kid it seemed like a mountain — and I'd start at the top of the hill, get going as fast as I could, and just fly off that knoll. It was pure sensation.

Hockey never gave me these sensations. My brothers, Bob and Mike, were both playing hockey when I was six. I signed up too, because I played everything, but hockey was just another activity. I played for three years, mostly house league, but I made one novice all-star team. That team played in the league against the Penetang team and the representative or "travelling" teams of all the other towns in the Georgian Bay area. I was taking group figure-skating lessons a few days a week and it really helped my hockey. In fact, skating was really the only thing I had going for me in the sport. In figure skating, you're moving backward most of the time, so my backward skating was better than anyone else's on the team. Naturally, they put me on defense. I remember the coach was a woman named Andrea Deschamps, and she thought I was going to be a really good hockey player because I could skate so well. She used to come over to our house to teach me how to shoot the puck. I wore one of those old leather helmets with a small band in front that covered the top of the forehead and another band about the same size in the back. Andrea had my stick taped in different spots to show me where I was supposed to hold it for various skills.

I wasn't really thrilled about hockey though, and when I decided not to sign up for it again when I was nine, I didn't miss it. Some figure skaters still play — Kurt Browning and

Jamiee Eggleton had their own team in the late eighties — but I never got the thrill from it that I got from other sports, so I gave it up. I didn't even see another hockey game until one night fifteen years later when I was training in Germany, met some hockey players and went to see them play for something to do. I still kept up with other sports, but I was spending more time figure skating. I was doing a wicked Russian split jump, which I taught myself, by just flinging myself into the air. I would abandon myself to skating. Every day when I came off the ice, my pants would be soaking wet from falling.

The North American sporting world has always felt a vague uneasiness toward figure skating. There lurks an underlying doubt: Is it a sport? Is it an art form? Or is it something else?

It is not a raging debate, but the questions do surface occasionally: when a newspaper columnist strives to make a point; when the crowd-pleaser is defeated, when an international judge is struck by a bolt of patriotic favoritism, even in discussions within the figure-skating community itself.

The most controversial issue is judging. Most other sports are quantitative: the team that scores the most goals wins; the first person across the finish line wins; the longest jump wins. Sports such as figure skating and diving, which rely on subjective judgments, are vulnerable to bias and error. And, because half the marks are awarded for artistic interpretation, the uninitiated may form the impression that this "sport" is more like a night at the ballet. The fact that music is such an important component of competition enhances the feeling. Until recently, compulsory figures played such a major role that by the time freeskating — the portion that television viewers can most readily appreciate — began, the final standings would be virtually established. It lent a whiff of predetermination to the final outcome. Television broadcasts do little to resolve the art-or-sport argument: figure-skating coverage is handled by sports departments with a production style lifted from entertainment.

The International Skating Union (ISU), the governing body of figure skating, has taken steps to meet some of the widespread criticisms. The school or compulsory figures have been gradually diminished in importance and will be eliminated in 1990. A radical new scoring system introduced in 1980 places greater emphasis on the relative standings of skaters in each discipline, rather than on how much one leads or trails by.

There should be no doubt, however, that figure skating ranks as a sport. The physical demands are extraordinary. Figure skaters spend more hours per day training than do athletes in almost any other sport. There are competitions that rate participants in order. Figure skating deals in spades the three cards that American sociologist Christopher Lasch says every sport must have: risk, daring and uncertainty.

Music requires interpretation. In order not to be dwarfed by his musical accompaniment, a World-class figure skater must not only execute tremendously taxing movements, he must make them look easy. Without music, figure skating would become a combination of speed skating and barrel jumping.

Some mainstream sports — boxing comes to mind immediately — also lean heavily upon judges' opinions. Even team sports, in which the object of the game is perfectly clear, require a referee's frequent interpretation of what is acceptable execution. Judging is a by-product of figure skating's technical nature. It takes a practiced eye to rate top-flight skaters.

Because there is no simple way to score it, figure skating is a complex sport. A number of different aspects of a skater's performance have to be taken into account when the three disciplines (figures, short program and freeskate) are marked: the difficulty of a program; how well the elements are performed; the style with which it is presented; the speed with which it is executed; the symbiotic relationship with a crowd. Wander into a group of skating connoisseurs and you may hear of a number of ways to rank the best. One individual will be swayed by artistry; another by the height and number of jumps; a third by the flow. But, *whatever their personal preference, knowledgeable skating fans usually agree upon the winner. The safety valve built into the system is that there is no single judge. It is always the majority of a panel of seven or nine that rules.*

There are mistakes in judging — often glaring ones — and inexcusable partisanship, but that should not affect the status of figure skating as a legitimate sport. As many important baseball games have been decided by an official's mistake as have figure-skating titles — probably more.

Of course, the vast majority of sports fans are males — although this is changing — and even if it is reluctantly acknowledged to be a sport, figure skating is still perceived as a girl's sport. Indeed, there are significantly more girls than boys registered in figure skating in Canada. Hockey is the sport of Canadian boys. There is a different television audience, too. Every boy dreams of standing at center ice in Maple Leaf Gardens with a hockey stick; not many dream of the same huge crowd watching their triple axels.

To a large segment of Canadian males, the idea of skating without a hockey stick is an anomaly. Something is missing. It reminds them of frustrating Sunday afternoons at the local rink. A few girls, the occasional boy and even fewer adults calmly circle the ice while fidgety boys and men, their hockey sticks jammed forlornly into the snow, huffily endure the required hours of "pleasure skating."

Not a particularly endearing introduction to figure skating.

I can't say that I never had any hassles from the kids at school. Almost all figure skaters in small towns encounter problems. There was one boy, in particular, who didn't like the idea that I was a figure skater: he would grab hold of me at recess and squeeze me in a headlock. He'd grind his arms into my ears and hold me bent over in the headlock for the entire recess.

I was going to the rink after school for group lessons. At that time my skates happened to be white. One day, when I was in grade four, I felt really brave and decided to go skating at the outdoor rink during the school winter carnival, wearing my white skates. Everyone was there. Before anybody could say anything, I whipped onto the ice and started doing a few tricks — skating really fast, turning some spins and doing some daring jumps. I figured that they'd give me a hard time, but that once they saw the skating, it wouldn't matter. And it didn't. A couple of the class clowns made their usual remarks; that was all. I was enjoying figure skating too much to worry about what my peers thought. The friends who really mattered accepted it.

The highlight of most club skaters' year is the club carnival. It is the lifeblood of the organization. As well as raising much-needed funds, it helps coaches much in the same way that a school concert helps music teachers, by providing a focus. It's easier to motivate students to learn new skills when there's a public occasion to show them off. Everyone in the club has a part in the carnival and the arena is usually packed with spectators, mostly relatives. There are production numbers in which the better skaters take the more difficult parts, and the learn-to-skates dress up as snowflakes, flowers or bumblebees. A few of the more accomplished club members are assigned solos and spend nervous weeks preparing for their time in the spotlight. And most clubs bring in a guest skater. Usually the headliner is someone who has done well at a recent competition, but occasionally he or she is a really big name.

When I was eight, I had my first solo in the Midland club carnival. One of the guest skaters was a twelve-year-old Torontonian named Vern Taylor, whose path I would cross again eight years later. Vern had just come back from North Bay where he won the bronze interpretive, a really big honor in those days. (The bronze competition was for up-and-coming skaters; silver and gold for older competitors.) In the interpretive competition, the skaters are all brought onto the ice where they listen to a piece of music three times. Then they return to the dressing room and think about the music. One by one, the skaters are then led back to the ice to skate their interpretation. The winner is the one, not with the most tricks, but with the most fitting interpretation. The emphasis, as with the second set of marks in the short and long programs, is on artistry.

We thought Vern was *it*. He was doing a half-axel, jumping forward and landing forward on two feet, and I remember picking up on it as he did it in his number. I started practicing the half-axel behind the backdrop while I was waiting for my turn to skate. I was going to take my Salchow out of my solo and put in the half-axel. In the end I chickened out, but it was a first step toward doing the axel.

After the carnival, we always had to hang around while our parents helped to dismantle the sets and clean up the garbage, but we didn't waste the time. Anytime I was at the rink and there was available ice, I was skating. So after a carnival, I wouldn't take my skates off and go home; I'd go back out for a skate. I'd be weaving in and out among the props while the crowd was still filing out of the arena. We'd do anything for a few minutes on the ice. We'd skate on outdoor rinks and ponds until it got too warm. We found a real windfall in the curling club. In April they turned their refrigeration plant off, but it would take three days for the ice to melt. I'd be out there the whole three days, skating on the increasingly wet ice.

The year after Vern Taylor was the guest skater, our carnival scored a major coup when Donald Jackson agreed to be the headliner. The club paid him $1500 to do the show and he donated $500 back to local skating. My mother was club president that year and my dad worked the lights. I'll always remember Jackson's jumping. He was amazing. We had a thick plastic backdrop so that if you were in the show, as I was, and waiting to go on, you could only see his silhouette, but I was still in awe of his performance. I remember trying to peek around the corner for a better look. It was the first time any of us had ever seen a world-class skater jump. My dad said later, "I pretty near swallowed my gum when I saw what he could do."

Every time a guest skater performs at a club carnival, some younger member is chosen to skate out to center ice after his number to present him with his gift. That particular year — I guess because I was a boy and because my mom was president of the club — it was me. After I gave him his gift I skated back toward the backdrop and, just before I got there, I leapt into the air and did a kind of cantilever jump, both legs together, and then disappeared behind the screen. If I was going to do it, I wanted to do it in style. Of course, the audience went crazy, which I loved. I was quite brash. In rehearsals before the show I said to Donald Jackson, "Well we've all watched you skate, now why don't you watch me skate?" He answered, "Sure, I'll watch you. Now, what can you do?" I did a few jumps and spins for him and he must have seen something he liked. He told my mother that I had talent and suggested to her that I take private lessons.

A few of the other skating mothers had already approached Mom to ask if I'd be interested in taking lessons. When Donald Jackson, whose name was synonymous with Canadian skating success, added his unsolicited support, the idea of taking skating seriously picked up momentum.

When the carnival was over, Donald Jackson left us with some autographed pictures and a whole new outlook. The autographed picture — "All the best, sincerely, Donald Jackson" — still sits on my shelf. In retrospect, that weekend was a crossroads in my skating career.

Donald Jackson played a large role in opening our eyes to figure skating. As a small-town family, we could have been overwhelmed by the enormity of big-time skating, perhaps considered it beyond our scope. We could easily have been satisfied with recreational figure skating.

However, buoyed by Donald Jackson's remarks, my mother decided that the time might be right for some lessons. She called a coach from Orillia who was picking up a bit of a reputation in the area. He made weekly stops in Midland. Mom asked him if he would mind having a look at me to see what he thought.

She didn't even tell my dad, but in the first week of March, when I was nine years old, I was scheduled for a fifteen-minute lesson with a fresh-faced twenty-one-year-old coach. The cost of the lesson was to be $3. By the time the 1988 Olympics arrived, the fee had risen to $44.

Even at that price, Doug Leigh is underpaid.

In 1973 a second arena would open in Orillia. Built to serve residents of the neglected south end of a city divided by a huge hill, railroad tracks and economic fortune, the arena was named "Twin Lakes" in honor of Couchiching and Simcoe, both of which lie less than a mile away. The Community Centre, the other town rink, stood on the hill in the older section of town. It had been completed twenty-two years previously, in large part through the volunteer labor of townsfolk and local foundry workers. The Community Centre is classic Canadiana: it battles bone-numbing cold in the winter, steamy heat in the summer. It can accommodate 2,300 spectators, but its high-backed wooden benches, lofty timber rafters and small ice surface give it a cocoon-like coziness. Twin Lakes, in contrast, was purely functional. With its block walls, low ceilings, metal rafters and small, tiled, lobby, it was meant to absorb the overflow of hockey from the Community Centre. At the urging of twenty-three-year-old Doug Leigh, it also provided off-hours ice time for figure skaters.

It had been Leigh's dream to own and operate a figure-skating school where rural and northern Ontario athletes could train closer to home, without having to deal with the culture shock of big-city clubs. In 1973, after four nomadic years in which he

peddled his teaching skills throughout the near-north, he opened
Mariposa School of Skating at Twin Lakes. Some locals doubted
that he could make a go of it, but since figure skaters rarely used
prime ice time — Mariposa rented the unattractive hours in the
early winter mornings, at midday, and in the spring, summer and
fall — the school went largely unnoticed by the general populace.
A hockey school owned by two Boston Bruins, Bobby Orr and
Mike Walton, also centered its on-ice operations at Twin Lakes.
Because of all the extra hours booked by Leigh, Twin Lakes
became one of a handful of rinks in Ontario to operate in the black.

By the time he opened Mariposa — a name derived from the
tales of humorist Stephen Leacock, who had lived in Orillia —
Doug Leigh was a driven, self-assured man, but it had not always
been so.

He was born in 1950 in Huntsville, a picturesque, rugged town
140 miles north of Toronto in the northernmost reaches of the
Muskoka vacation area, close to Algonquin Park. Huntsville is a
hockey town, and Leigh, who is still an ardent Maple Leafs fan,
played on the town all-star teams right through peewee (age
twelve). His aunt, Marilyn Leigh, taught figure skating, and Doug
Leigh took up the sport to improve his hockey. Unlike his future
star pupil, he never faced the scorn of his peers. A number of
players took up figure skating. "I had nothing but support from
my friends, even through high school," Leigh recalls. "Maybe
because I grew up with a pair of hockey skates in one hand and
figure skates in the other. Sometimes I'd be switching them for
practices half an hour apart. The hockey guys would say, 'Do one
of those crazy jumps for us'."

Leigh quit hockey at twelve to concentrate on skating and
would spend summers in North Bay, studying under Austrian
Hans Gerschwiler, the 1947 World champion. At the age of
sixteen, Leigh finished second in the national junior championship to David McGillivray. He did a triple loop, toe loop and
flip. "There were only a few of us doing triples, but nothing else —

*we were as boring as wallpaper." After this silver-medal perform-
ance, Leigh suddenly retired. "I quit because I had no confidence,
none at all," he said.*

*He threw away his skates and finished high school, during
which time he started a small construction business. At age
seventeen, he was hiring local students to help him build houses,
and his confidence began to expand with the business. He had
acquired the carpentry skills, and motivation, from his father,
Bob. "He owned his own construction company and I used to see
how hard he worked. Up till 2:30 in the morning doing drafting,
and up again at 6:30 to meet the work crews. And he had time for
everyone. He used to drive me up to North Bay, which was a
hundred miles away, for lessons, and have me back for school, and
then he'd go to work all day." A strong parallel to the relationship
between Brian and Butch Orser.*

*In 1969 Bob Leigh died of a perforated ulcer, and Doug's
grandmother told him that his father didn't want Doug to have
anything to do with the construction business. He wanted him to
get back into skating. So Doug bought a new pair of skates and
took a job with the Orillia Figure Skating Club. He began his
professional career in the cold, damp Community Centre and was
soon supplementing his income by travelling all over central
Ontario — Midland, Elmvale, Barrie, Huntsville, Bracebridge —
tutoring skaters. "I was like the Flying Doctor, making house
calls. Eight rinks in a week," he quips. He was already building a
reputation as a good teacher when Joanne Orser telephoned him
about her son. "He was just like a colt out of the barn, really
rambunctious," says Leigh of Brian Orser. "He was fast, pretty
quick in his stroking and, whether he knew the names or not, he
was doing Russian split jumps and single flips. It was a very
acrobatic style. He was like a thoroughbred. Someone left the barn
door open and there he went."*

*Leigh is given to figurative speech. It is one of his most effective
teaching tools and his off-ice conversation is peppered with*

similes and metaphors. He is an admitted workaholic. Skating is not only his vocation, but also a business, and his school has grown significantly, partly due to Brian Orser's record, mainly due to Leigh's hard work.

He does have a lighter side, however. His passions include hockey and navigating his huge boat across lakes Simcoe and Couchiching. Leigh loves the "toys" that his hard-earned success has brought him. He has the latest in video and stereo equipment. He lives in a magnificent, modern house, which he shares with his fiancée, Michelle Simpson, who, along with Brian Orser, was one of his top students in those early years. She was a third-place finisher in the national novice championships before a debilitating Achilles tendon injury ended her competitive skating. She then began a new career as a successful figure-skating coach.

Leigh laughs easily but also possesses a sharp tongue. He is a stern, stubborn taskmaster. Brian Orser almost left Doug Leigh at least twice in his career. Then-national champion Tracey Wainman had a terrible fight with him during a lackluster training session on New Year's Eve, 1981. Leigh cannot abide a lack of commitment. He is a fighter. In the late seventies, he fought and won a battle with skin cancer.

Leigh's school was successful and, by the 1980s several other towns, among them nearby Barrie and Newmarket, were hoping to lure him away from Orillia. Because conditions in the south-end rink were deteriorating, and the city was slow to respond, Leigh began to listen to offers. When an edgy city council reversed its decision to build a new rink, Leigh initiated his move to Barrie. In 1988, his final season in Orillia, there was some name-calling. Sadly, the relationship between the town and the skating school ended in bitterness.

In the mid-seventies, however, Doug Leigh was still determined to put an unsuspecting Orillia on the world figure-skating map, with Brian Orser as the key cartographer. Ironically, the town fathers have always seemed a little prouder of Gordon

Lightfoot and Stephen Leacock, both of whom left Orillia to seek their fame and fortune, than they have of Orser and Leigh, who came to town to seek theirs.

I can still remember that first lesson with Doug, the first private lesson I'd ever had. He was upbeat, friendly and smiled a lot, but I knew instinctively that he wouldn't take any nonsense. A lesson with Doug began on time and you got your full fifteen minutes' worth — you still do.

Doug wanted to see what I was capable of so, as I did with Donald Jackson a couple of weeks before, I showed off a little. I did split jumps all over the rink. Then we settled into the lesson. We worked on centering a corkscrew spin, one of the basic, but most visually effective, moves in figure skating.

One thing that really stuck in my mind, and is reflected in my skating to this day, was his description of "momentum." That was a big word for a nine-year-old kid. In fact, I didn't know what it meant. But he used an example I could relate to — throwing a ball. He said, "You don't just pick up a ball and throw it. You have to get some speed up, get you arm moving quickly, then release that ball out of that arm. That's momentum." I understood clearly. That kind of communication is the basis of a good student-teacher relationship and Doug has always had that skill. In later years, when I worked with kids in seminars, I tried the same thing to explain momentum, but it just went in one ear and out the other.

It was discovering, through Doug, the concept of momentum that made that first lesson so memorable. I can still recollect every detail of that day: the smell of the arena, what Doug said, everything.

We signed up for weekly private lessons with Doug and my skating quickly began to improve. One acquired skill led into another. Doug would take a flip jump, for example, that I was doing without really knowing its name. He would break it down into separate elements, such as the entry, midair position, increasing rotation speed and landing. We would work on it until I did it technically correctly, and then we'd move on to the next jump.

There are six jumps in skating, differentiated by the direction you're going when you take off, what edge of the blade you use, and whether you use the toe picks. Some skaters, like Toller Cranston, jump with a clockwise rotation. Most, however, jump to the left, or counter-clockwise, as I do. A *toe loop* is probably the simplest jump. You take off on your right back outside edge, dig in your left toe pick to help with the takeoff, and land on the back outside edge after the revolution. It's also called a "cherry" or, if you make a small turn before the entry, a "toe-walley." On a *Salchow*, you jump from the back inside edge of the left foot to the back outside of the right, without a toe pick. If you do that jump with the aid of your right toe pick, it's called a *flip* — a jump I struggled with later in my career. A flip that takes off on the back outside edge instead of the inside is called a *Lutz*. A Lutz is especially difficult because you're trying to counter your natural body movement. Your approach is in a clockwise direction, but you execute the jump counter-clockwise. To do a *loop* you take off and land on the same foot and edge — the back outside edge of your right foot. The only jump you enter facing forward is the *axel*. You take off on the outside edge of your left foot and come down on the outside edge of your right.

The degree of difficulty increases in proportion to the number of revolutions. The first triple jump wasn't landed in World competition until Dick Button, an American who is still a fixture on the World scene as a commentator, did a triple loop in 1952. Donald Jackson did the first triple Lutz. Another Canadian, Vern Taylor, did the first triple axel, and I did the second, third and fourth.

A skater's body build and personal preferences determine the jumps that are the most suitable for him. Generally, the axel is considered the hardest and the Lutz second most difficult. The toe loop and Salchow are usually the first jumps a skater will master.

I don't have many distinct memories of jumping in those early years when I was nine, ten and eleven. I recall doing toe loops, Lutzes, Salchows and flips. I remember jumping high and falling a lot. We never used a harness in those years. Doug had one later, but I didn't use it until 1985, when I was experimenting with the back flip, which I use in show programs. I never hurt myself learning the jumps, at least not until I was fourteen, when I broke my right leg three times in fourteen months.

Doug opened new doors for me in figure skating. He introduced us to René Brunot's skate sharpening shop in Thornhill, north of Toronto. Figure skates take special sharpening, and René was the best. You could buy used skates in the basement of his shop and that's where I got my first pair of black skates. John Knebli makes excellent skates. Once I discovered them, I never used any other kind. In the early days, though, all of my skates were second-hand, including the Kneblis.

Doug also opened the door to off-ice training, and off-season skating, notions I had never considered, but which I adopted wholeheartedly.

After a few lessons with Doug, I tried my preliminary figures test. It was held on April Fool's Day, 1971. I passed, then went to spring school in Orillia. The spring school was held at the Community Centre, which was cold and quite damp — most of the rinks we worked in were like that.

After the carnivals for club skaters, the testing stream is another focus of activity for Canadian skaters. After you pass your preliminary figures test, there is a series of eight progressively more difficult tests of figures. Once or twice a year a club will have a test day with CFSA-accredited judges marking your performance.

At the fourth test figure, the competitive and test streams divide. You may be content to become a "test skater", passing tests, as in a Red Cross swim program, and forgoing competition. If you want to be a competitive skater, you must pass a test for each level of national competition — novice, junior and senior. Basically, you're trying to show skating officials that you're ready to compete at that level. Each competitive-level test also requires that you pass a certain figures test. There is a similar testing pattern in dance, which I was also studying, with Doug's associate Tom Harrison.

At the end of April, having passed my preliminary figure, I took my first figure test and — an omen of things to come — I failed. In fact, on the same day at the Community Centre, I also failed my swing-dance test. It was hard for a nine-year-old to take. I cried my eyes out.

After spring school, Doug went to North Bay to spend the summer teaching, but my parents wouldn't let me go. They agreed to allow Mary Kay and me to enrol in summer school at the Dunlop Street Arena in Barrie, which was about thirty miles away. I passed my first test there. Mary Kay and I were given a new scribe — which you use to lay down a sample figure to trace — and were both so proud that we fought to carry it. I also landed my first single axel that summer in Barrie.

My parents and the other three kids spent the summer at our cottage on Georgian Bay. Because we were skating, Mary Kay and I moved in for three weeks with Doug's aunt, Marilyn Leigh, at her cottage in Victoria Harbour, near Midland, and we'd ride in every day to Barrie with her and Judy Manley, a skating mother.

The next summer I talked my parents into allowing me to go to North Bay. It was a bigger and better summer school, but I got a healthy dose there of what the rest of my adolescence was to be like if I stuck with skating. We went to the rink before we even found the house where I was going to stay. I skated at the rink, everything was fine, and then we drove over to Norma Peltier's house, where I would spend the summer. It came time for my parents to leave and, while I didn't want to see them go, I think my mom was more upset than I was. My dad said he looked out the rear window as they pulled away and never saw such a forlorn sight as this ten-year-old boy standing on the porch waving goodbye. I was really homesick. I cried my heart out all night, and all the next day at the rink. My parents called that day, and I told them that I wanted to come home. They said it was too far to come up right away. They knew that I would soon get over it. And I did. I met friends at the rink — fellow skater Robert Tebby from Huntsville was there. Mrs. Peltier had a pool in the backyard, so I could swim and dive after my five hours at the rink each day. In fact, when the summer was over, I wanted to stay. Every goal-oriented athlete has to endure this kind of experience at some point. In skating, you go through it a lot earlier than, say, hockey, because you have to be making your mark by the time you enter your teens. No matter how you slice it, though, ten is awfully young to make this kind of career decision. My parents visited me every second weekend that summer. I'm just glad they didn't come and get me when I begged them to, or I'm sure I would never have been World champion.

I entered my first competition that summer, at Hyland Arena, in Scarborough. It was held in two parts — a freeskate and the bronze interpretive.

I could do a double Lutz by then, but I missed it in the freeskate. I don't remember being nervous, but I had never competed before, and I scrambled around the ice. I lost contact with the music and I think I even forgot a portion of the program. I know I finished fifth, but I don't remember who else who was in the competition.

After the freeskate, we all went out and they played the music for the bronze interpretive. We then went back to the dressing room and waited to be called out to interpret the music.

In those days, I was terrible at interpreting music, so I just went out and did all the jumps I'd missed in the freeskate. I just wanted to compete. I came eleventh and was really upset because I'd landed all the jumps.

My parents had come along to watch and they were concerned for me. They asked somebody if the judges wrote comments down and, if so, could they see them to figure out why I finished eleventh. That showed how naive we were about skating — you just don't do that kind of thing.

After that summer in North Bay, I came back to Midland, went to school and skated all fall and winter at rinks in the area. We didn't have to go back to North Bay because, by the following summer, 1973, Orillia had built a new rink and Doug had a summer school there. We bought a trailer and parked it in Tudhope Park, close to the rink, and I lived there in the summer with Mary Kay and my mom, on the shores of Lake Couchiching.

Things didn't change much for us when Doug moved his school into Twin Lakes Arena, at least not immediately. I still went to school full time, except one half-day every week, when I skated with Doug at Elmvale or Midland.

I'd skate some mornings before school, almost every day after school, at night, and much of the day on Saturday. I also skied at Mountainview whenever I could. We were skating at several rinks in the course of a week. Skating became a lifestyle. I'd come home from school, grab my skating bag, my mom would start the car and we'd be off. Some days, the weather would be horrible, but we never turned back unless the roads were closed.

I was progressing fairly quickly, but Doug was a demanding, stubborn coach. He required me to do everything so often that when it came time to do it in a competition or test, it would come automatically. This approach led to our first big blowup, when I was eleven years old.

We were working on my third figure. He was making me do a first-test serpentine and it wasn't very good. Doug got mad because it was only a first-test figure and he started to make a big thing about it. I thought it was weak because I hadn't worked at it much. I got just as mad and said "Go to hell!" and stomped off the ice. I phoned up Tom Harrison, Doug's associate, and said, "I want you to teach me." That didn't go anywhere. Doug made an issue of it, and I couldn't come back until I apologized to him. Although our coach-skater relationship is the longest in current amateur skating, it hasn't always been a bed of roses. We are both perfectionists. Over the years, we have learned how to deal with each other, and although we're different in many ways, we are close friends. Spending thousands of hours on the ice together, we have had to be.

About the time Twin Lakes opened, we moved from Midland to Anne Street in Penetang. I was in grade six and switched from St. Mary's school to Corpus Christi. The house was much bigger — we had our own bedrooms — and sat up on the hill about a block from the Coke plant and right behind the Penetang Arena.

That house and that arena represented a benefit of small-town life that you could never reproduce in a city, unless you had unlimited money and influence. The arena manager was a man named Ron Marchildon, who is now the town's recreation director. He gave Mary Kay and me a key to the arena. Every day we'd get up at about 5:30 in the morning, make ourselves some toast and climb over the back fence to the arena. We'd unlock the door, turn on the lights and skate on our own — "patch" (compulsory figures) and freeskate — for two or three hours. Then we'd climb back over the fence, make some more toast and head off to school. We would have a nice fresh surface for these predawn workouts because, after the last hockey game each night, Ron would flood the ice. Sometimes, he'd even show up in the morning and flood it. All at no charge. He was moved by our dedication. When the Wintario system of funding was started he applied for, and got, one of the first grants from the Ontario government. The $500 grant was for Mary Kay, Michelle Simpson and myself, and I think we used it all to buy lessons.

There could be no substitute for the ice time Ron Marchildon gave us. Ron provided me with the figure-skating equivalent of those legendary frozen ponds, where young hockey players develop their own feel for things, and squeeze in the extra hours that eventually take them to the NHL.

In those early days, I was blessed with another skating asset, although I didn't recognize it as such. When Doug taught me a new jump I would go home that night, lay in bed and try to get a mental feel for the basic elements of the maneuver. My body twitched while, in my head, I'd try different moves until I got a feeling that I knew would work. Once I felt that I had grasped the sensation, I couldn't wait until the next day to try it out. At the rink, it was as if my body had already made the jump and knew exactly what was expected. It was just a matter of confirming the feeling on the ice. Nine times out of ten it worked.

More than ten years later, when I started to work with Dr. Peter Jensen, a sports psychologist, I would find out that as a young boy I had accidentally stumbled upon "mental practice," one of the most important forms of preparation.

In a similar vein, I used the tiled floor of our big rec room downstairs at Anne Street to imitate on-ice programs. Whenever CTV would telecast a skating event, during every commercial, I would be stimulated to put music on the record player and do spins and jumps and footwork across the slippery floor. I'd continue for hours after the show was over.

That first year on Anne Street, some of this extra work and thought began to pay off. I was twelve years old when, in early 1974, I entered my first sectional competition in the prenovice division, at Leaside Arena in a Toronto suburb. When you're a prenovice, your competitive season ends with the sectionals. Novice, juniors and seniors continue on to divisionals and nationals if they do well enough. I finished last among the five skaters in figures, won the long program (there is no short program in prenovice and novice) but only moved up to fourth over all. Paul Martini — who later shared a World title with his pairs partner Barbara Underhill — finished in the medals in that competition.

Although I missed the podium, I did catch the eye of the Canadian Figure Skating Association through its technical director Barbara Graham, who would become a close and valued friend. I was invited to the national seminar in Vancouver that summer.

That seminar was as far from home as I had ever been, and the occasion of my first airplane flight. Now I've flown enough miles to earn my pilot's wings.

I was the youngest skater at the seminar. A number of good-natured practical jokes were foisted upon me by the older skaters — Gordon Forbes, Kevin Hicks and several others. First, they took the door off my room in our dormitory at the University of British Columbia. They could walk in at any time and, one night, after I'd gone to sleep, they snuck in and moved my clock ahead seven hours. I had the alarm set for 7:00 A.M. so I could be up for the first session. When it started to ring, I hopped out of bed and went down the hall for a shower. When I came back to my room, dripping wet, there were the older guys, killing themselves laughing, because it was only midnight. It was all in good fun, the kind of thing that builds camaraderie in a sport marked by so much drudgery in daily practice.

The next year, I won prenovice sectionals and was fortunate in that the 1974-75 season was a Canada Games year. In winning the sectionals, I was selected to compete in the

Ontario Winter Games at Thunder Bay in December. Michelle Simpson was also chosen and we two small-town kids — me from Penetang, her from tiny Elmvale — were sort of the "stars" of Simcoe County.

I won the Ontario Games, landing my first competitive double axel in the process. Lloyd "Herbie" Eisler, who did a wild Toller Cranston interpretation, was second. I advanced to the Canada Winter Games in Lethbridge two months later. That was a huge thrill for a thirteen-year-old, partly because I was given my first team uniform: a Hudson's Bay coat with real fur on the collar, a cardigan bearing an Ontario emblem and a white lambswool hat.

My parents drove to Toronto International Airport early in the morning where I met Doug and the rest of the team for the flight to Lethbridge. The living accommodations during the Games were innovative — we were bivouacked in a school in which desks had been replaced by bunk beds. In our class-room-dormitory were Ontario's men figure skaters and the volleyball team. Among the skaters was Kevin Parker, who skated a classification higher than I did, because he had passed some tests I hadn't. He won Men's A and I won Men's B over Neil Giroday and Quebec's Ghislain Briand, respectively. Briand became a close friend of mine when he spent summers training in Orillia a few years later.

There was no figures competition, just a two-and-a-half-minute freeskate, which, with twenty-five guys, must have been difficult for the judges. I landed another double axel and finished first on all five judges' cards — quite an achievement for a skater they'd never heard of.

It didn't click in my mind that I had won a national competition. I was only thirteen and was more impressed by the number of good athletes there were in Canada and all the fun we had.

When I got back from the Lethbridge Games a few of my friends — Kevin St. Amant, Michael Leclair, Pete Dumais —

— decorated my house with handmade posters and had a congratulatory party for me. The town had a little parade for me. At the curling club, where I had squeezed in extra skating time on the melting ice, there was a small ceremony and presentation. The school gave me a merit award. This established a new tradition there of honoring a student who achieved something major outside of school. It was to be an annual event and was given in my honor. It was the first time anything was named after me and I still go back to Corpus Christi to present the plaque to the year's winner.

A few months later, I graduated from elementary school and prepared to start at Penetang Secondary School. Reflecting the French heritage of the town — explorer Samuel de Champlain had spent his first few Canadian winters there — the school was later renamed École Secondaire Penetanguishene.

Penetang is actually a French-speaking town, but I don't remember any French-English problems as I was growing up. I couldn't speak French, apart from the little we learned as part of the school curriculum. When I finished grade eight, my dad tried to get me to take it over again, in French, at St. Josephe. I told him he was out of his mind. My buddies are going to high school and I'm going to take grade eight over again? I'd have to be crazy. I picked up French and German in later years, because I trained and travelled in Europe so often, but I still don't speak French as well as I should. I can understand both languages much better than I can speak them.

I registered for grade nine at Penetang Secondary School in the fall of 1975, but figure skating was really starting to interfere with "normal" schooling. I had won the Canada Games and was about to embark upon the tough grind of sectional, divisional and national competitions. I was soon going to have to make some sacrifices that others my age would not. Among these sacrifices was a formal education.

2. Broken Legs and Triple Axels

Skating didn't interfere at all with my first term of high school. It's pretty difficult to figure skate when you're lugging your right leg around in a plaster cast.

The leg was actually broken in July during summer school at Orillia, but for two months I ran a gauntlet of disbelieving health professionals. In 1975, sports medicine hadn't developed to the stage it's at now, especially in the small towns. Today, the break would have been diagnosed, put in a cast and therapy prescribed immediately.

The leg was originally injured when I dug my pick into the ice for a double flip. The pain was excruciating and I took a few days off. But the ankle didn't swell very much, so I eventually resumed training. There wasn't much pain on the landings, but any toe jump, in which I had to put pressure on the leg for takeoff, was torture. I complained a lot and even missed the summer competition in Ottawa.

The initial diagnosis was tendinitis — an inflammation of

the tendon sheath of the upper ankle. I saw doctors everywhere, including Toronto, but no x-rays were taken. In fact, we were told by one doctor that I was just looking for sympathy.

In the end, it was a physical therapist at the hospital in Midland who discovered what was wrong. He suspected a fracture because the ankle wasn't responding to therapy. He arranged for an x-ray and discovered a vertical break at the ankle. Right away, I went into a cast, beginning an eighteen-month epic of plaster of paris and emergency rooms.

The upshot was that I didn't have as much trouble with the early-going in high school as I would have in the following two years. In fact, I made the honor roll in grade nine. History was one of my best subjects because of the excellence of the teacher, Larry Banks. His main subject was physical education and he knew I was serious about my skating. He encouraged me throughout my high-school career, which was fairly brief. I had support from some other teachers as well, although others were distressed by my subsequent poor attendance.

I did well in math. I also excelled in geography, appropriately enough, since I would see so much of the world over the next decade. One subject that troubled me was science. I hadn't done well in grade eight, so I registered in level ɪv, not the advanced course. But on the first day of class, I went to the wrong classroom and found myself in level v. I was so embarrassed, I didn't want to say anything to the teacher, so I stayed there the whole year. That's how shy I was. In fact, I was shy through most of my amateur skating career. It was only in the final couple of years that I felt that I could "work a room" full of reporters or businessmen, and not stand in the corner like a wallflower, or lean on someone else for support.

I got back onto the ice in November and had to work very hard to catch up. It was my first year in novice and there was a good chance to advance to the nationals in London. But since 1975-76 was an Olympic year, all the competitions were moved ahead by a couple of weeks.

At sectionals in late November, I finished second to John Belec, and advanced to the divisionals in December at St. Laurent, Quebec. For the first time in competition, I landed a triple jump, the Salchow, and won the event. Barb Underhill was there, and she recalls watching me, and being thrilled by the triple Salchow and double axel. I went home to prepare for my first Canadian championships, which were slated for London in January, and was relishing the thought of the competition and landing more triples. By this time, I was missing two afternoons of school each week to train, as well as taking time off for sectionals and divisionals. On one of those Tuesday afternoons — December 17, the day before my fourteenth birthday — I met Doug at Midland Arena for our weekly freeskating lesson. Coming down from a double axel, I broke my leg again.

I felt it go. It didn't hurt as much as the first time and I didn't cry. I was driven over to the hospital for an x-ray and then my father drove me to Toronto to Sick Kids Hospital. The break was much worse this time and the leg had to be reset.

I woke up in the recovery room, wearing a cast that extended from my foot to well up my thigh. There was no dramatic moment when I asked if I could skate again. . . . I knew in the car that my season was over and that I would miss the Canadian championships. I went to London to watch anyway, because Michelle had qualified in ladies' novice.

I was very depressed about not skating in Canadians, and I developed a severe case of hives. My dad called them the "ticked-off hives" because they were probably related to my disappointment. I had them on my leg under the cast and on my face — my eye was swollen completely shut. However, attending Canadians as a spectator gave me a sense of what the national championships were all about. I think it helped to smooth the way for me the next year. Then I only had to deal with myself, not the overwhelming nature of the huge competition, where more than two hundred athletes are entered in various divisions.

I got back onto the ice in March, in time for spring school in Orillia, but wasn't allowed to jump because the stress would have been too much for my right leg. I could practice figures, though, and by April I was allowed to freeskate, but just stroking. I was very impatient to get back to jumping. At that point in my life, the jumps were the essence of skating. Stroking and figures didn't offer anything close to the same sensation.

The idea struck me that if coming down on the right skate was the big problem, I could get back into freeskating by jumping the other way. The majority of skaters, including me, rotate counter-clockwise on their jumps and spins. But there have been some excellent skaters who rotate clockwise. It's a matter of what feels natural.

I started to experiment with a loop jump because, clockwise, you take off and land with the left leg. At first, things felt awkward and distorted in the air. But then I began to be more comfortable with the opposite rotation. I started to train seriously, instead of simply playing at something out of the ordinary. I worked myself up to double Lutz before I was able to resume landing on my right foot and discard the reverse jumping. The experience compares to a right-handed baseball pitcher having to throw with his left hand for a month. Even now, I can do an axel and double Salchow the other way, although I don't work on it. Once in a while I play around with it.

I somehow managed not to break my leg again for a full year, which at least allowed me time to win the 1977 Canadian novice championship.

If it comes as a shock to people that in 1977 I finished first in the compulsory figures when I won the Canadian novice championship at Calgary, it will be more jolting to hear that I actually like, and respect, compulsory figures.

So do a lot of other top skaters. Gary Beacom, silver-medallist, and some other top skaters defended figures in *Canadian Skater* magazine, arguing that they develop proper skating technique. Toller Cranston, an outspoken critic of figures, would not agree, of course, and I don't think the general public would either. Under pressure from that public, the ISU eliminated figures three months after I retired.

As I was growing up, I didn't understand figures, but as time went on, I came to like them. The problems I had in figures had nothing to do with lack of work, but I only occasionally grabbed the real feeling of figures. Sometimes I'd have it — as I did in 1977 and in 1987 and 1988 — but I could never hold on to it as I did with the sensation of jumping. Aleksandr Fadeev had it, even though he usually practiced his figures on two feet, his "free" leg helping support the other skate, which cuts the figure. But when competition came, he had the feeling.

Figures require incredible coordination. I never had a problem with that. But there's a certain feeling you get in which everything, from the bottom of your skate blade to the top of your head, acts as one. Your pulse has to be really low. As in the case of a pistol shooter, anyone can squeeze the trigger, but it's the centering and aiming that is difficult. Centering is important in figures, too. It's almost as if the blade of your skate is your eye and you have to focus through it to the ice.

The blade has to be like a magnet on the ice. Some skaters like Fadeev and Josef Sabovcik can skate like that. Even if the body is all over the place, the foot is anchored like a rock. If I wobble my body, my blade wobbles. And if I'm really nervous, these faults show up more.

In figures, you have to lay down the necessary pattern on

the required foot. It's very important to get the first cut down correctly and symmetrically. Then you trace over it, the number of times depending upon the figure. They cut the number of tracings in half in the eighties, which made it a little tougher to cover mistakes.

Figures are nerve-wracking because of the incredible concentration required. Doug compares the tension to that experienced by a diamond cutter sitting over a precious stone. In my final two years, I felt that my figures had peaked, and mentally I knew exactly where I was every second on the ice. In other years, I'd get ahead of myself. All of a sudden I've done the turn and it's happened before I can even think about it — a mistake. Then I'm at the top of the circle and I'm too far off and the mistakes snowball. Many skaters, including Donald Jackson in 1962, have had this problem with cumulative errors in figures. I overcame it in the final years with help from Jimmy Grogan of California, and Czechoslovakia's Karol Divin, the man who had finished second to Donald Jackson.

I don't think that Canadians, me included until the final two years, understand how much attention has to be paid to figures before they can be mastered. We go through the motions. We spend time on them, but not the quality time. When I did begin to focus — working with a scribe to draw the figure, like a compass, checking and rechecking, getting fresh ice every time, taking each tracing very seriously — I started to do well. I realized that that's what Europeans do. They concentrate on figures for four hours each day while we wait for freeskating practice. We've had isolated successes. Tracey Wainman loved figures. When she was on patch, you couldn't talk to her, she didn't bring her head up for a second. I learned almost everything I knew about figures in the ten years after I passed my gold figures test, and a lot of people think that after they pass that test they're qualified to teach figures. I've also seen figures traced under real stress at the World level and I know what comes apart and what doesn't. What doesn't unravel is the essence of good figures, and it takes a long while to learn that essence.

In 1977, I didn't skate terrific figures. I didn't win a single figure, but came out on top because I was consistent. It was the last time that I would win a national figures competition until 1985.

Everyone was nervous that year. A guy would win one figure, then completely botch the next one and tumble down the standings.

I had only finished third at divisionals, but in Calgary I won the long program too, landing a triple Salchow, triple toe loop and a couple of double axels to win my first national title. My footwork was developing, but the spins lacked a little bit. I wasn't very flexible back then, so the camel spins weren't too attractive. I didn't know what to do with my arms, and being shy, I didn't look up at the audience even once during a program. For me, it was a matter of doing triple jumps and double axels and some stuff in between.

I was elated when I got my medal. Michelle finished third in ladies' novice and I was thrilled about that. It was an exciting week for the Mariposa School of Skating. We stayed in the Palliser Hotel in Calgary and did the usual kid-stuff things — running through the halls, yelling and hanging around.

My mother was with me that year, but my dad stayed at home because my mom and I got so edgy before a competition. Even in novice, you're affected by tension, because skating is a pressure-packed sport. It's you and you alone for five full minutes (four and a half since 1982) and your whole season rests on that performance.

Everyone gets nervous. A lot has been made in the media about me and nerves and pressure, but I don't think I was affected more than anyone else. Only in one year, 1986 at Geneva, did I have a big problem with nerves. Over all, I think I dealt with the immense pressure fairly well.

When I got back from Calgary, Penetang had another little parade for me and I started to gear up for junior competition. It would be the first year I would have to do a short program, in which the ISU prescribes the seven required elements — spins, jumps and footwork — and the skater selects the music and designs a two-minute routine. Skating began to take an even bigger bite out of my life. By now I had abandoned midseason skiing and all other sports until after divisional and nationals were over.

And, of course, I broke my leg again soon after I got back from Canadians.

It happened when I was competing in interclub competition. This was to help out the Midland Figure Skating Club in the South Georgian Bay competition against clubs from Owen Sound, Collingwood, Elmvale and Barrie. For the third time in a year and a half, I found myself in a cast.

When I was able to resume training, it was necessary to work on a short program, a whole new set of figures and to continue to improve my freeskating. I had developed a triple Lutz and was doing it in both the short and long program. People were going crazy over that, because it was a difficult jump for a junior skater. Not many seniors were landing one. I won sectionals and divisionals and headed to my second Canadians, in Victoria.

I was second in the figures, fell on my double axel in the short, and finished third in the long to finish third over all. So I actually dropped positions after figures, one of the only times that ever happened.

Dennis Coi won, and Daniel Beland was second, but Beland was too old to go to junior Worlds, which is for skaters sixteen and under, so we all knew that finishing third would get us on the Canadian team. It was close between Kevin

Parker and myself, but I got the bronze and the berth on the team.

Despite my on-ice successes, I was up to my neck in academic trouble.

I was missing a lot of school. Three full days a week I was on the ice, meaning I was only at school for two full days. First term wasn't bad, but once the winter training schedule started in late October, I had to put figure skating ahead of my studies.

Aside from the training, I missed almost the whole week for sectionals, divisionals and nationals. Naturally, the bad marks started to increase. In most of my classes I was lost, but I managed to scrape through grade eleven.

After all these years, I can still remember the drop in my marks in second term. I went from 90 percent to 37 in marketing. In math I tumbled to a 41. I passed English and geography and my physical-education teacher, who wasn't even aware that I figure skated, gave me an NM — no mark. Typing was a disaster — 17 percent, the only subject I ever failed, because I brought all the other marks up in the third term.

I got my grade eleven, but at that point I had to make a career decision. Teachers were upset that I wasn't attending class, I was having trouble catching up, and it was only going to get worse. In another year I would be in senior competition. I was now skating more than eight hours a day and beginning to travel internationally. I decided to drop out of school.

I only needed four credits to get my grade twelve, and I registered to take them one at a time, by correspondence. I found I couldn't do it. Surprisingly, considering how hard I work on training on and off the ice, I didn't have the discipline for correspondence school. After getting good marks on the first five or six lessons, I dropped the course and still don't have my grade twelve.

While I was still attending Penetang Secondary, I had junior Worlds to deal with. Just before I went to Mégève,

France, for that competition, I decided to go to Ottawa to watch the 1978 World championships, to check it out, just in case I ever made it that far.

In 1978, the World figure-skating championships were held in Ottawa, only the third time Canada had played host to the world's best. It was a memorable week for a number of reasons. The previous year's Worlds had been held in Tokyo and, as did the 1985 Globals held there, they lacked excitement and sparkle. But the Ottawa Civic Centre is the perfect building, in the perfect community, for a World figure-skating championship. Attendance is never a problem and the organization committee is a well-oiled machine. Ingeniously tucked under one set of stands at Lansdowne Park, a football stadium, the arena is not perfectly symmetrical. Above the lower bowl, there are no seats on one side. Instead, a slanted, tiered ceiling reminds you that you're partially covered by a stadium. The effect is to magnify sound, particularly cheering, as it sweeps around the bowl.

There was plenty of cheering in the week of March 7-12, 1978: Soviet pairs skater Irina Rodnina tied the legendary Sonja Henie's record of ten consecutive World titles, but in the other three disciplines the defending champions were dethroned. American Charlie Tickner parlayed superb choreography into the men's title over one of the strongest fields ever, with 1977 champion Vladimir Kovalev dropping all the way to fourth. The men's final, however, is best recalled as the day the first triple axel was successfully landed in World competition.

The axel is named after a nineteenth-century Norwegian skater, Axel Paulsen. The move, which he pioneered, requires the skater to turn so he enters the jump facing forward off the outside edge of one skate, rotate in the air, and land on the outside edge of the other skate, facing backwards. A single axel — the highest, and most graceful of single jumps, and still favored by Brian Orser and other top leapers as an artistic move — is actually one and a half revolutions in the air. A triple axel is three and a half *revolutions in midair. The landing surface is one edge of a blade, which itself is only three millimeters wide. The maneuver generates enough torque that if the non-landing or "free" leg does not counterbalance the spin, severe bone damage can result. The jump requires a great deal of speed, excellent spinning power and a high muscle-to-body-weight ratio. Not everyone has the skill, or courage, to attempt it. Little wonder, then, that sixteen years after Donald Jackson introduced the first triple Lutz, and thirty years after Dick Button landed the first double axel, the axel still remained the final frontier among triples.*

Vern Taylor, who celebrated his twentieth birthday only ten days before the 1978 competition, made the breakthrough when he successfully, if somewhat shakily, landed the triple axel a minute into his program. Taylor, runner-up to Brian Pockar at the nationals, was buried in the middle of the pack after a truly Canadian finish of fifteenth in figures and a disappointing twelfth in the short program. With the axel he was seventh in freeskating and twelfth over all, one spot back of a young American making his world debut, Scott Hamilton.

Taylor forms an interesting bridge between Jackson and Orser. Jackson had landed the Worlds' first triple Lutz. In 1973 Taylor, then a novice, landed the first triple Lutz in a Canadian competition. His shaky triple axel was perfected by Orser, who made it his personal trademark on the way to the World title. Ironically, it also cost him two other titles. Taylor was coached by the venerable Sheldon Galbraith, who had pushed Jackson over the top.

Taylor's achievement, difficult as it was, never attracted the level of publicity that surrounded Button and Jackson, because their breakthroughs were accompanied by World titles. Still living in his home town of Toronto, he is remarkably blasé about his historic leap:

"Two other skaters tried it before me in Ottawa. They weren't successful, but I didn't know that when I went out there. I had worked on it for about eight months. I used hip pads to protect my right side from falls. I didn't have it in my mind that I needed to be

the first, but I was determined to land it. I enjoyed the challenge. I completed the jump just seconds after a triple Lutz. It wasn't landed with grace, or real style, but it was a clean triple axel. When I did it, some of the judges didn't even know it was a triple axel. Some said it wasn't until they played it over and over on replay. I don't think they were expecting it. There was no way I wasn't going to do it. At Canadians, I had overrotated it and put my free leg and one hand down. When I landed it at Worlds, it kind of came as a shock: 'Hey, I'm still standing.'

"I certainly heard the crowd yell, but soon forgot what I just did because I had four more minutes left."

One of the nine thousand-plus who roared for Taylor after the triple axel was sixteen-year-old Brian Orser. He would successfully land one himself the following year and would refine it soon afterward. It would be 1982 — when the Austrian Thomas Hlavik landed one at the World championship — before anyone but Orser landed a triple axel in competition.

"It was a matter of people realizing technique," Taylor says. "Once they see how it's done, then everyone can copy it. Brian established the balance, the awareness, what his feet were doing, the proper height. The way he's built, he is capable of maintaining that spin rotation and slowing it down. Plus you have to have explosive muscles."

Taylor, who was plagued by injuries in the following season, never landed another triple axel in competition.

I cheered heartily for Vern when he came down from the triple axel, though I wasn't really sure that he had landed it successfully. At Canadians a few weeks earlier I had one in my program, but I never really got into it and bailed out of the jump. Vern tried it the next night in the senior long program, overrotated it and landed on two feet with his hand down.

In Ottawa, the axel was a little shaky and he did a little three-turn afterward, so I didn't know if they credited the jump. Later, after countless video replays, it was announced that Vern had broken the triple-axel barrier. I was surprised to find that I was very disappointed.

When I was learning triple axels, I can honestly say I never thought about being first in the world to do one. Learning it was just another step in the progression of triple jumps. I'd learned the first four, then got the triple Lutz, which was the biggie in those days, and Doug just had me go on to a triple axel. Doug recognized that I could do one because I'm short and light and have narrow hips, plus my technique in taking off and landing was good. It didn't really take me long to get the axel in practice. I didn't understand at the time that I was breaking new ground. To me, it was just a new jump, and Doug didn't dwell on it. Being first was never an issue.

But once I started landing axels, I remember people being shocked, and everyone wanting to see it. I think because there wasn't anyone else, other than Vern, trying it, I gained a reputation as nothing but a jumper. I deserved it at the time, but it was hard to shake after I'd added other elements to my skating.

I don't have any vivid memory of landing my first axel in practice. I know that it was at Twin Lakes. When you're working on a new move, you come close so many times that there is very little physical difference between the jump that just misses, and the first one you actually land. Doug, perceptive as usual, recognized this very early. He started to pay his students for making a jump the first time. You had to do it when he said, and the subject never arose until you were nearly there, but it was still an out-and-out bribe.

I think I got five or ten dollars for that first triple axel, but I remember my first single axel more vividly. That was worth only a quarter in those days. Doug put the quarter on the side of the boards and said, 'it's yours if you land it.' I understand that the old Maple Leafs coach, Punch Imlach, used to do something similar to motivate his players during the Stanley Cup playoffs. He would dump money on the dressing-room floor and tell the players that this was the amount they were playing for. Doug is a big Leafs fan, so there may be a connection. I landed the axel at Barrie and when I did, I skated by and picked up that quarter. I was ten or eleven at the time and I proudly slipped it between the top of the boards and the glass to the lobby, where my mom was watching. It wasn't the money, but what it symbolized, the work and all the falling . . . and taking it off Doug gave me a wry satisfaction, too.

A week after Worlds, I was in Mégève, France, for the junior World championship. It was my first international competition and it was the first time that my parents paid for Doug to go abroad — setting a precedent that would last throughout my career. If Doug wasn't an official team coach, then my parents sent him. He never asked for much. In fact, at some places he crammed into a single room with my parents and me, a long way from the glamor some outsiders associate with figure skating. Doug took a financial beating in lost lesson fees at home while he was at a competition with me. My dad's reasoning was so typical of him: "You wouldn't send the Toronto Maple Leafs into Boston without their coach would you? You wouldn't ask someone else to go behind the bench. Doug goes along."

In Mégève, I finished eighth in compulsory figures and second in the short, to move up to third behind Dennis Coi and Vladimir Kotin. I telephoned my parents and my dad told me that if I skated a clean program, I would be third, no doubt about it. I asked him how far it was to Mégève, and he said he didn't know exactly. Then I said I didn't know either, but it was too far to come not to go for it.

So, I tried the triple axel, butchered it and did poorly the rest of the way to drop to fourth. Moving up to pass me was a fourteen-year-old American named Brian Boitano. Brian had been seventh in figures and won the short, but somehow was still fourth heading into the long program. We were skating under the old total-points marking system, and Coi finished first with 170.86 points, Kotin was second, and Boitano had 163.74 to edge my 162.64. Under a new marking system ten years later in Calgary, the score would be even closer — a tenth of a point.

Dennis's gold, along with a pairs win by Barb Underhill and Paul Martini and a silver in dance from Kelly Johnson and Kris Barber, helped Canada to a team medal.

I didn't win a medal, but that competition had a lasting effect on me because I forged some strong friendships. Brian Boitano and I are still close, despite our heated competition. Barb, Paul, Kelly, Kris, Dennis, Lloyd "Herbie" Eisler, and I became a tight-knit Canadian unit. In the eighties, many of us travelled together regularly as part of Canada's World team. Paul and I were roommates at the World championships four years running, from 1981 to 1984. That group has drifted apart, but Barb and I are still very close. After she and Paul won Worlds in 1984 and turned pro, I missed her a lot. Before the 1988 Olympics she phoned me one night, very worried, wondering how I was handling the pressure. She said she could remember what she went through in 1984. She gave me some very positive advice — to just skate for myself.

About this time, the decision was made that I would move to Orillia. Since I wasn't going to be attending school, it made sense to live close to the rink where I would be doing the majority of my training.

I moved in with Greg and Judy Myles, who lived near Lake Simcoe and only half a mile from Twin Lakes Arena. A few months before, I'd passed the exam to obtain my driver's license. Now I could transport myself from rink to rink, or at least travel with Doug, who lived down the street from the Myleses.

It was difficult to leave home, but Penetang was only half

an hour from Orillia and since my dad's company serviced that area, I'd see my parents, brothers and sisters often. Sixteen is the age at which most hockey players are forced to leave home to pursue their careers, and I guess there was no difference in my case. In fact, most figure skaters do it a lot sooner if they're from small towns. Because I considered Doug so knowledgeable, I didn't have to make that lifestyle decision as early.

Although I was living in Orillia, there was still a lot of travel. We had ice time at several different rinks in the snow-belt; our route formed kind of a triangle, each side thirty miles long. We'd usually skate at Orillia every day, beginning at about 6:00 A.M. with patch. But that rink also was committed to school classes and hockey games and practices so we also booked time at Elmvale, Barrie, Stroud (where Greg Myles taught), Midland and Penetang. Quite often we'd be at three rinks in a day, crawling through severe snowstorms to reach them. Usually there would be only Doug, Greg and I in the car, but as the school grew in later years, there were others with us.

Much of the time, conditions would be less than ideal. I can remember having the odd session at Coldwater Arena, just off Georgian Bay, between Midland and Orillia. There, the snow would sometimes drift in under the door of the rink and onto the ice, and we'd have to shovel it off. Some of the other rinks were very, very cold, especially for early-morning patch. Twin Lakes was always damp and cold until Doug and his skaters raised money and obtained a Wintario grant in the mid-1980s to buy heaters. That made a huge difference. The ice wasn't as hard — figure skaters usually like a softer ice than hockey players because it helps to grip the blade on takeoffs and landings — and we didn't have to bundle ourselves up in so many cumbersome clothes, either.

Doug had video-replay equipment at Orillia. This is an

invaluable aid in jumping. It can be the start of "visualization", that is, the process of watching yourself do something correctly enough times to make an imprint on your mind. As time went on, he upgraded his equipment, and an off-ice training room with weights, ballet bar and mirrors was added. Even in the late seventies, we spent much of the summer-school time working off ice with fitness trainers like Nancy Rosewarne and, later, Jim Parker. Thanks to Doug, and with some help from the City of Orillia (again, at Doug's persistent urging), it developed into a complete package, one that I could probably not have duplicated anywhere else.

So, in this period, I was closer to the rink; I was travelling in the car with Doug two or three times a day and talking figure skating with him; and I was enjoying extra ice time during the day. Consequently, my skating became more consistent. I won both sectionals and divisionals in my second junior year.

I headed for the Canadian championships in Thunder Bay, where I had won my first big title, at the Ontario Winter Games, four years earlier.

At Thunder Bay, Barb and Paul added the senior-pairs championship to the junior title they'd won in 1978. They were only the third pair in the history of Canadians to win those titles in consecutive competitions.

I was still trying to win the junior championship that year and I didn't do myself any favors with a ninth-place finish in figures. I had gone from the penthouse of winning the novice figures in 1977 to the doghouse of ninth two years later. I completely blew the rocker and didn't know how to recover. I was stunned and my nervousness carried over into the double-threes, which wandered everywhere. Then I just said to myself, "To hell with it", and went out and did a good loop, which saved my day.

Kevin Parker, who was my main rival at that time and had

beaten me consistently when I was younger, finished fourth in figures. Considering that he was an excellent freeskater, he was in a pretty good position to win the junior championship.

Kevin moved into first place after the short program, but I vaulted to second from ninth by winning the short. I did a double-flip-triple-toe-loop combination.

In the long program I included two triple Lutzes, which was a major accomplishment, but that wasn't what had the crowd buzzing.

After the first triple Lutz, I landed a triple axel.

It was my first competitive triple axel, the first ever done at Canadians at any level and only the second in history. The axel was a squeaker, but it was clean. I didn't go very far across the ice. I spun like a top and had to really bite in on the landing, which I whipped out of quickly, but I kept on skating backwards to maintain the flow. It was a clean triple axel, finally. What an exhilarating sensation! The axel, plus the two Lutzes, gave me the junior championship of Canada.

The axel was the talk of the town. It was the novelty of the skating world. There were huge headlines. People would flock to the practice sessions after I won, just to see me land a triple axel, and I would oblige. I have to admit that I loved it all, but it was also during this period of euphoria that I realized that people would expect the triple axel now, and that I was bound to it.

That championship resulted in one of my two long-standing superstitions. (The other is putting my left skate on first). Lisa Kinnear, a girl from Midland whose father, Guy, is a trainer with the Toronto Maple Leafs, was trying her junior bronze dances and I was partnering her through the test in Penetang. When she passed, she gave me a little red and pink bear. I still had it in my skate bag when I did the triple axel and won, and it became a good-luck charm. I've changed skate bags countless times, but have this ragged, dirty toy in my bag even now.

After winning the junior championship, I was listed for my first international senior competition in the last week of September. Canada had entered the Vienna Cup sporadically since it started in 1974, generally sending women's teams. The Vienna Cup was designed to give graduating juniors and first- and second-year seniors a taste of international competition.

Within the Canadian Figure Skating Association (CFSA), there were many who doubted that I was good enough to enter the Vienna Cup. I had to take a test at the Toronto Cricket, Skating and Curling Club in Toronto on a warm August day. I think it was the first time I'd ever been there and I was apprehensive. This was the bastille of Canadian skating: Barbara Wagner and Bob Paul had skated there; Donald Jackson and Petra Burka, too. I wasn't really nervous, but I was a little overwhelmed. It was a plush setting for a teenager who was accustomed to cold, damp hockey rinks. The Cricket Club had chandeliers in the lobby. Some of the roofs of the rinks I skated in leaked.

I had to do figures and my long program in front of David Dore, who was then head of the CFSA's technical committee. The figures were laid down on the curling rink — it was the first time I'd skated on curling ice that wasn't melting — and then we moved over to the skating rink for my long program. I skated well. David Dore passed me on the test and recommended me for Vienna.

Around this time, I ran headlong into a quandary that has faced all skaters with potential: I was put under pressure to move to an established skating center. There had traditionally been only a handful of skating clubs that could consider themselves to be "finishing schools." Usually the veteran international coaches — the Sheldon Galbraiths, Ellen Burkas, Louis Stongs and other excellent talents — were headquartered there, and they attracted dozens of skaters who'd shown promise to their clubs. Ottawa's Minto, the Granite, Cricket Club, Vancouver North Shore and a few other big-city clubs were, by long-standing practice, acknowledged as the only places to develop and hone the skills necessary to advance to the World-championship level.

A few days after I was cleared for Vienna, I received a curious letter from the CFSA. They were proposing a trade: Kay Thomson would come north to work with Doug; I would go to the Granite Club to work with Louis Stong. The letter said I could benefit from working with Louis, and I eventually did work with him at the Granite Club in the 1980s.

But it was an obvious shot at Doug. I guess some people within the CFSA felt I could do better, that Doug had no proven track record. It was almost like that dilemma of not getting your first job because you don't have any experience.

I showed the letter to Doug and to my parents. Doug got very mad; in fact, he was seething. He took the letter and I think he still has it in his files. I was angry, too. The letter hardened my determination to stay in Orillia and eventually win the nationals. We both knew there was a lot we didn't know, but we were determined to learn it all. I knew that Doug was good, and we'd been successful together, especially that year. People who didn't deal with him every day didn't recognize how well he worked with me, how he knew my moods, when to push me, when to let off. And his teaching was technically sound: I knew that, because I was also studying everything I could about skating.

I have to admit I was also a little afraid of the big city. Whenever I went there I felt like a nobody. I was intimidated. I didn't like the feeling of being a very small frog in a very big pond. I never felt confident enough to abandon the small-town atmosphere, and everything it had to offer, until I won the World championship.

There were other little digs over the next few years, but Doug and I were determined to do it our way. In the end, I think we were vindicated. Now, small-town skaters not only come to places like Orillia (or Barrie, since Doug has moved) but they sometimes stay home a little longer, as good local coaching develops, partly through CFSA-sponsored coaching programs. The mountain is coming to Mohammed.

I went to the Vienna Cup and won it, although the field didn't include anyone who stuck with skating for any length of time. I finished second in figures, which broke new ground for me internationally. The Vienna Cup was my first real taste of senior international competition. I remember sitting outside my hotel room, talking to skaters from seven or eight different countries, comparing notes about our native lands and talking about the world elite — Jan Hoffman, Robin Cousins, Charlie Tickner, Vladimir Kovalev and all the others. The junior Worlds had been an international event, but the Vienna Cup put me against other seniors. Winning it, and landing a triple axel, made an impression on World judges which would help pave my way when I did make the Canadian team a couple of years later.

I moved into the senior ranks in the 1979-80 season. With sectionals in Orillia at the Community Centre, I had to skate only an exhibition program — my long program — because there were no other senior men. At the divisionals in Markham, I finished second to Gary Beacom, which was a little disappointing.

Again, it was an Olympic year, so Canadians at Kitchener were held a little earlier than usual. I finished fourth in figures, which elated me. Just twelve months earlier I had been ninth in junior figures. But I had a disastrous short, missing my double-loop-triple-toe-loop combination.

I was third in the long program, despite trying and missing my triple axel twice. There was only one triple axel planned for the freeskate, but I missed it the first time. Later in the program there was a slow part scheduled. I didn't care much about artistry or program flow, and as the program went on, I felt that I had to land a triple axel. I had nailed one in junior and now it was expected of me, so I just scrapped the slow section of the program and zoomed around the ice to set up the axel. I missed that one, too.

Still, it wasn't a bad showing for a first-year senior. I finished fourth behind Brian Pockar, Gordon Forbes and Gary Beacom. My season was over. Pockar, who had won his third consecutive national title, represented Canada at the Olympics, then Worlds where his top-ten finish (ninth) gave Canada two men's representatives for 1981.

After the Lake Placid Olympics, the International Skating Union (ISU) instituted a radical, and long-awaited, restructuring of the marking system. Canada fully supported the revision.

The basic principle of the system was that a skater's relative position in each of the three disciplines — not the total of his marks for the three sections — was used to determine the final result.

The three segments were factored: school figures were worth 30 percent of the final mark; the short program, 20 percent of the final mark; and freeskating, 50 percent. At the end of each discipline, a skater was assigned a number of penalty points, arrived at by multiplying his standing in the discipline by the corresponding factor.

As in a golf match, the skater with the fewest penalty points won. A perfect penalty score of 2.0 required a skater to win figures, the short program and free skating. He would have taken 0.6 figures points (his position [1] times the figures factor [0.6, which is 30 percent of 2.0]; 0.4 short program points (1 × 0.4); and 1.0 freeskating points (1 × 1.0). A skater who was second in all three disciplines would have totalled 3.0 penalty points ([2 × 0.6] + [2 × 0.4] + [2 × 1.0]).

If there was a tie in penalty points, the result of the freeskating discipline was used to break it. That was another principle of the system — superior freeskating prevailed.

It is important to remember that, under this system, the mark was not a judge's full comment on the performance. If, for instance, a skater received 5.4 from the Italian judge and 5.7 from the u.s. judge, there was not necessarily an Italo-American feud brewing. The Italian may simply have been a lower marker. If the next skater received 5.5 and 5.8 from the Italian and the American, respectively, and the following skater 5.6 and 5.9, the two judges would have marked the three skaters exactly the same — third, second and first. It was the relative standing that counted.

The standing in each discipline was determined by a majority decision. If a simple majority of judges placed a skater first on their cards — even if the majority was one vote — he finished first. The same applied to all positions. If no skater had a majority, other rules came into play, such as "the most placings of second-or-better."

The system that the new accounting replaced used a majority system, but for the entire event. In other words, points carried over from discipline to discipline. A good freeskater could be too many points behind in figures to catch up by exploiting his specialty. It's possible that Donald Jackson would have won the 1960 World title if the new system had been in place.

Under the new system, then, a skater who finished fifth or tenth in figures would be simply that. He would not be fifth and seventy points behind (or second and forty-five points in arrears, as Donald Jackson was in 1962). This change reaffirmed the commitment of the ISU to school figures but continued the steady decline of their impact. This decline will, of course, be complete when figures are eliminated in a couple of years.

The Canadian Figure Skating Association decided to apply the new international scoring system to the senior division at the national championships, beginning with the 1981 event at Halifax.

At the time, a lot of people thought that the new scoring system helped me to win my first Canadian senior championship. They were wrong. It wasn't the change in the way competitions were scored, but a major change in the way I trained for them that was the significant factor in my winning the national title in late January 1981.

Doug and I have continually grown in our approach to training. With each new development, we realized how little we had once known about figure skating. It wasn't until the spring of 1980 that we discovered runthroughs.

Before that, we only occasionally went through a program from beginning to end during practice. It was rare for us to run through a full program even twice a week. We would work long, hard hours on elements and portions of the program; we engaged in serious off-ice fitness sessions; but we thought it was natural to be very fatigued near the end of every program during a competition.

That began to change when our choreographer, Suzanne Russell, came up to Twin Lakes Arena to design the program that summer. In the second week of summer school, she started making me do complete performances of my program, from beginning to end. I thought she was crazy.

In the fall, Suzanne would meet us in Barrie once a week and I dreaded it because I knew I'd have to do my full program. But it made me work harder. It was difficult at first. Gradually, however, it got easier, until finally, it became a snap to run through a demanding five-minute program every day. For the first time in my life I discovered what skating shape was, and I really haven't lapsed out of that condition since — except for my one-month holiday every year.

I had two international competitions during the off-season: St. Gervais-Oberstdorf and Skate Canada. The European competition was skated in two parts during late August, one in St. Gervais, France, the other at Oberstdorf, West Germany, on the following weekend. I won the French event, beating Norbert Schramm in the process, then finished second in Germany to Tom Dickson, an American. I know my success in that competition was due to superb conditioning.

On the last weekend of October, I went to Skate Canada in Calgary. It was the first of six occasions that I would compete in Canada's fall international.

It was a challenging event, perhaps the best men's field ever assembled for a Skate Canada. There was Scott Hamilton and David Santee of the United States who would finish one-two at the following Worlds; Canadian champion Brian Pockar; French champion Jean-Christophe Simond; Brian Boitano and myself.

I was fifth in figures, ahead of Brian Boitano and just one spot back of four of the world's best. But I missed my combination in the short program and fell on a triple Salchow in the long, even though I landed the triple axel. I finished sixth. Scott Hamilton was great in winning ahead of David Santee and Brian Pockar.

There was not much thought in my mind of beating Brian Pockar for the national championship because he was ranked ninth in the world.

There was even less thought of beating him a couple of months later when I broke my hand. My sister Mary Kay had been away skating with Ice Follies, and came home to Penetang for Christmas. We hadn't seen each other for five or six months and, excited to be together, we were outside just goofing around after a heavy snowfall. I decided to jump off our TV antenna, down ten feet into a three-foot pile of fresh snow. When I let go of the tower, my mitt froze to the metal and I plunged straight down onto the patio, with my hand breaking the fall. We went out that night to a local pub, and by the end of the evening my hand was throbbing. The next morning, I went to the hospital, found out it was broken and had a cast put on my lower arm.

With my arm in a cast, I couldn't even try the triple axel,

because everything has to be so precise. At divisionals, I did everything but the axel and skated very well. At the end of the program, I noticed David Dore and Louis Stong standing and applauding me.

After divisionals, the cast came off and I started training the axel again. I remember skating in Barrie's Dunlop Arena at eight o'clock in the morning when it was thirty-below inside the rink, and I'd be burdened by a hat, mitts and layers of clothing and still do the full program, triple axel and everything. That's the kind of energy I had that year.

Nationals were in Halifax. I started off on the right foot, so to speak, with three strong figures. I finished second to Brian Pockar and ahead of Gary Beacom, who had a big name in Canadian skating. A good short program, in which I also finished second, followed. My combination was triple toe-double loop and I actually finished first on three of the seven judges' cards. That made me very excited, but I wasn't even thinking about winning. I just thought, "Wow! Look how close I came to him."

Sometimes, memory becomes self-editing. Things seemed to be so easy when I was younger, that I tend to remember difficult times in my life as if I had just sailed through them. But, to this day, I recall exactly how nervous I was in Halifax. I was so uptight before the short program that I almost threw up. I remember telling that to Barb Underhill. It wasn't much different before the long program on the following night.

I was nervous, not because I wanted to make the World team, but because I had raised my standards significantly that season and had been training so well. I wanted to skate as well as I had been practicing.

And that's just what I did.

Brian Pockar skated before me. I didn't know it, but he had over-rotated a triple Salchow and a double axel. In fairness to Brian, I should mention that he had slashed an ankle in a training accident and missed a great deal of practice time in the fall. His conditioning was off, while I was in the best shape of my life.

My long program tore the house down. I did a superb triple axel and everything else was as clean as a whistle. In the middle of my performance, I could see Debbie Wilkes interviewing Brian on CTV, something they normally only did with the winners. I had already landed the axel and thought to myself, "You're going to be interviewing me in a few minutes."

The crowd exploded when I did the axel. Even before I finished the program they were on their feet. I ended the program with a flourish and I remember being so excited when I was done. Then the marks came up, five of them 5.9s, but I didn't know if I'd won because I didn't understand the new scoring system.

Then Michelle Simpson came running up to me, crying and yelling, "You're Canadian champion! You're Canadian champion!" Michelle's father, Larry, is a figure-skating accountant and I asked him, "Is it true? Is it true?" as he hurriedly tried to put all the marks together. He wasn't certain, but said he thought I'd won, so I raced around the boards to see the computer at the other end of the ice. And that confirmed it. I had won six of the seven judges and was Canadian champion.

I went into the dressing room and cried silently, strictly out of joy. It wasn't even a dream come true, because it happened before I had a chance to dream about it. It was like winning a million dollars without a ticket.

I cried uncontrollably on the podium, but I wasn't embarrassed at all. I looked into the audience and there were so many people crying along with me. David Dore was crying. Barbara Graham was crying. David said that I had done it a year earlier than he thought I would.

It was a trying time for Brian Pockar. He had been a popular champion, but he handled the loss with class. He did mention in some newspaper articles, though, that under the old scoring system he thought he would have won. Dr. Suzanne Francis, one of our top judges, wrote a letter to *Canadian Skater* magazine to say that this analysis was wrong, that a judge will use the scoring system in such a way that the skater he or she thinks is best wins. And if I did win because of the new scoring system, well, I lost a much bigger prize — the 1984 Olympic gold medal — on that same system. But I do think a lot of people thought the scoring system favored me.

I partied all night with Rob McCall, who'd won his first championship with Marie McNeil, and with Barb Underhill, who'd won her second pairs title with Paul Martini. The song "Celebration" was big then and it seemed appropriate. We danced to it at a disco, and later there was a party in my parents' room. Kelly and Kris made the World team, as I did. Barb and Paul and Tracey — all the kids from the 1978 junior World team, plus Brian Pockar, a World-team veteran, were also at the party. It was a great year for Doug, because Tracey Robertson from Orillia, another of his students, also won the novice title.

We went to Worlds in Hartford the next month. I laid down some good figures, but only finished ninth. Here was a new dose of reality to face — you pay your dues in your first couple of years at the World level. Barbara Graham, however, was ecstatic that I was as high as ninth. What bothered me was that I was quite a ways back of Pockar, who placed third, and in my insecurity I thought people would say that I shouldn't have won Canadians.

A solid short program got me sixth in that discipline and moved me up a little. Despite being very nervous, I skated a strong long program, although not quite as good as at Canadians. I landed the triple axel, which elicited the expected reaction from the biggest audience (about 15,000) I'd ever skated in front of. I doubled a Salchow, so I ad-libbed at the end by taking out a double toe loop and putting in a triple Salchow. I was fifth in the long, to finish sixth over all behind Scott Hamilton, David Santee, Igor Bobrin, Fumio Igarashi and Jean-Christophe Simond. Brian Pockar didn't skate well in either the short or long, and dropped to eighth. I learned later from the *Orillia Packet and Times* that my sixth-place finish was the best-ever debut by a Canadian male.

Just before the long program, though, there was a disturbing incident. American broadcaster Dick Button, who had won four World championships and an Olympic gold, came up to me just before the warmup and said brusquely, "Some of my sources tell me that your triple axel is cheated." I looked at Doug and Doug looked at me and we just kept on walking. We said to each other, "Do you believe that guy?"

Dick gave me bad press as recently as 1987. He said that in the men's event there is no artistry. Shortly after, they showed some tapes of the years he won the Worlds. In an interview I laughed and said, "Have you seen *his* tapes?" He got wind of it and he apologized to me at the Olympics.

In any event, I got a standing ovation at Hartford, and the triple axel made a big impression. People came out to practices just to watch it. I think it got me noticed much sooner than I might have been, and helped to propel me quickly up the skating hierarchy.

After the competition, I was shocked to be asked to join the International Skating Union tour through the United States and Canada. How much of a small-town kid was I? I didn't even know there was a tour.

The tour is a reward for skating at the World level. After eleven months of predawn sessions on patch, drafty arenas, sore muscles and nerve-wracking competitions, it's a chance to skate for skating's sake, to strut your stuff for an appreciative audience, without pressure. The tour travels across the continent in which the World championship was held. It draws big crowds in large arenas, playing off the recent publicity that the top skaters have received. Along with the medal winners, some other top finishers, good exhibition skaters and rising stars are asked along. It's like the highest level of club carnival you can get, with everyone skating at least one solo.

Top skaters all prepare innovative exhibition programs for shows and tours, using artistic and crowd-pleasing tricks and costumes they can't risk in competition.

Eventually, I became one of the big attractions on the ISU tour — I designed my back-flip especially for it — but in 1981 I had no grasp of the concept. Luckily I had some exhibition music with me, but I wasn't much of a show skater. I wore a competition outfit, didn't know what a sequence was and felt intimidated by what everyone else was doing.

I was completely naive about playing an audience. I would go out and do a triple axel and a triple Lutz — moves that would drive a crowd crazy in a competition. On tour, however, the crowd would clap politely and crane their necks to look for the next skater. Then Norbert Schramm would come out wearing a headband with wings on it, and the crowd would go nuts. Or Scott Hamilton would come out and do a chicken number with not a single jump in it. It was the corniest thing that I'd ever seen, but in front of 19,000 people, it worked. I learned a lot, especially about show biz, by watching Scott Hamilton.

The best thing about a tour is that you spend three weeks with other skaters, people who've gone through what you've gone through just to get there. After a dozen years of doing little else but skate, the athletes become the people you can most identify with. It's gratifying to get to know them — especially the Russians — as people, not just as skaters.

One of the skaters who travelled on that 1981 ISU tour was the diminutive, newly crowned World champion Scott Hamilton, then twenty-two years old.

In the emerging era of spectacular jumpers who included Brian Orser, Jozef Sabovcik, Grzegorz Filipowski, Brian Boitano and Aleksandr Fadeev, Hamilton managed to win four World championships by never doing more than three different triple jumps. But Hamilton was a sound technician, with whispered takeoffs and landings, and blinding footwork speed. He was the prototypical all-round figure skater that the ISU had in mind with its new scoring system: he was good at figures, solid technically and possessed of a riveting artistry. He had the steely concentration of the consummate competitor and was able to remain focused on his task despite the enormous pressure of being the favorite every year, and therefore over-hyped by the zealous u.s. media.

When Hamilton was five, the native of Rosemont, Pennsylvania, was stricken with Schwachmann's syndrome, an illness that affects the intestines and induces malnutrition. He battled the disease for four years, and was cured, but Schwachmann's left its mark. He never grew past 5 foot 3, 110 pounds.

Skating proved effective therapy for the disease — he called it accidental therapy rather than intentional — and he remained with it. He studied under the legendary Carlo Fossi, but ended up with Don Laws, who coached him to his Olympic and four World titles. Hamilton was the first quadruple winner since fellow American Hayes Alan Jenkins in 1956. His family didn't have much money, a drawback in American skating, but a sponsor provided him with the backing he needed to pursue his career.

Hamilton preferred not to mention his childhood disease, but it was too gripping a story for the world press to pass up, especially during the 1980 and 1984 Olympics. He considered it over-dramatizing.

He was an excellent World champion, never lording it over the other skaters. He was blessed with great tact. By 1983 he was *telling the Canadian media that he feared Brian Orser's improvement, and in 1984 he said he was convinced he couldn't beat the Canadian another year. It was a gracious comment, but it was also based on truth. In 1984, Orser won three of the four non-figures events at Olympics and Worlds. It was the first time that anyone had outskated Scott Hamilton internationally since 1980.*

I was a big Scott Hamilton fan. Every year on tour, I would never miss his performance. During a lot of the other skaters' performances, I would sit in the dressing room, just waiting my turn or recovering from my show, but whenever Scott skated I'd go out and watch. He had a wonderful light touch, was very expressive and his footwork was dazzling. He liked my skating, too, and I think that he was a little envious of it, in a good way. He wished that he could do some of the things I could do, and I wished I could do what he could do. We became very good friends and shared a lot of laughs on tour.

The Russians were a lot of fun. When we travelled in North America there was sometimes a KGB agent or two riding right on the buses with us, to watch over the Soviet athletes and guard against possible defections. I remember one of them: he was about 6 foot 4 with a gold tooth, just like a James Bond villain. But he was a good guy. And the Soviets always had an incredible supply of vodka. Everywhere we'd go, a bottle of vodka would appear.

Igor Bobrin, who won the bronze medal, was on that tour and he was hilarious. His show program was one of the most memorable in skating history. He satirized his own Mutt-and-Jeff pairs teammates with a mime in which he had an invisible partner. He'd whip her all over the place and, after one particularly energetic throw, our lighting director would send a spotlight up into the audience searching for her landing place. He'd be called for encore after encore.

The great Soviet dancers Andrei Bukin and Natalia

(Natasha) Bestemianova are the gems of the sport. Natasha portrays herself on ice as a vamp, but she's really like our Tracy Wilson — she just loves people. They're very warm and very sincere. They hug you a lot. Natasha and Igor Bobrin eventually married, but at that time they were sneaking around, seeing each other. On a tour, you always keep an eye out for budding relationships between skaters. There are one or two each year.

Aleksandr Fadeev joined the tour a year or two later. Aleksandr is a very inconsistent skater. He can be excellent. One year — 1985 — he put it all together from beginning to end, and was outstanding in winning NHK, the fall international in Japan sponsored by the NHK communications company, and the World championship. We kept our distance from each other because we're both very shy, not because we don't like each other. Every once in a while he'd get a bit tipsy and this smirk would appear on his face, so that he'd look almost like a little boy.

Norbert Schramm was on tour and he and I just didn't hit it off. I have to admit that I was a little jealous at times, because he beat me a couple of years and I didn't think he was that talented. But after he retired, we met in a bar in Paris for a good, friendly talk, and there was no competition at all between us, as there had been when he was an amateur.

Brian Boitano joined the tour in 1984. At first, he was pretty shy, a typical all-American athlete I guess. But every year he seemed to come out of his shell a lot more, and we developed a strong friendship. We took a lot of the pressure off each other. I'd see him at a competition and we'd joke about the situation. A bizarre sense of humor is just one of the things we have in common: we're also both interested in owning restaurants; we've both kept our original coaches right through our careers; and we think the same way.

Brian is a very consistent skater. It amazed me that night after night he could do the triple Lutz, and the other jumps.

On a tour of twenty cities he'd miss maybe two triple Lutzes. In the 1988 Olympic year, he made big steps, Sandra Bezic helping him find a direction and meaning to his skating.

Jozef Sabovcik was another good friend. In fact, in the summer of 1983, I sent letters to the Czech skating federation requesting that he come to Orillia to skate for the summer. Jozef was a lot of fun on tour, but he lived the good life a little too much, and had terrible training methods. If he had trained properly, Brian Boitano and I would have been in big trouble, because Jozef had so much natural talent. He just didn't have the discipline. He won Europeans three times, but won only one big medal — the Olympic bronze in 1984. By 1987, he was out of skating. He married another close friend, Tracey Wainman, and they now live in West Germany.

I roomed with Christopher Dean of Great Britain that first year and both he and Jayne Torvill were just regular skaters. The three of us even took in Disneyland together. But, by the next year, they had become famous with their "Mack and Mabel" routine and were much more aloof, almost as if they were royalty. Their skating was marvelous, probably the best there's ever been, but they began shutting the rest of us out.

Another skater I watched every night was Denise Biellmann, whom I absolutely loved. In fact she was my favorite skater before Katarina Witt came along.

My friendship with Katarina started on that tour. Our careers ran parallel, although she had more success than I did when she won two Olympic gold medals. She always wanted me to win. She and I have known each other since we were teenagers. By 1985 we were very close. A crowd of us — Katarina, Jozef Sabovcik and three Canadians, Katerina Matousek, Herbie Eisler and myself would go dancing. We'd have to sneak her out some nights because her stern coach, Frau Jutta Mueller, wouldn't let her go. And we'd have to sneak her ice cream whenever Tom Collins, the organizer of the tour, would pull the bus over to buy us banana splits or sundaes.

In her final year, she talked a great deal about her skating career. It was really quite sad because, in East Germany, once you stop competing you don't skate any more. That was breaking her heart. Now she's taking up acting and apparently her government has reversed its policy, and she'll be able to come out for a few shows. I'm really hoping that she and I can skate together as professionals. We were talking about it one night. She leaned over and said, "When you do a show, please don't forget about me." She almost cries when she talks about it. How could anyone forget Katarina Witt? She has earned so much respect in the skating world, and I'm going to miss her.

Tour serves a number of purposes. It gets us ready for professional careers, gives us a little money — we received $150 each for a show in 1981, double that by the time I left — and it lets the tension of the season wash away.

All skaters on tour are World-class athletes. We took care of ourselves, but there was still a lot of partying on off-days. One night in Montreal, Rob and I decreed that the party would be in our room. We had efficiency rooms in the motel and we made a rule that everyone had to cook a dish from their own country and bring it to our room. The Russians brought borscht; the Germans brought Wiener schnitzel; the British brought crêpe suzette — maybe they always wanted to be French — the Americans made piggies in a blanket and pizza. Robert and I made lasagna and Caesar salad — not too Canadian, but we didn't have any moose steaks.

It was a marvelous party and people still talk about it. The laughter was oiled a little by the eight bottles of Dom Pérignon that Tom Collins sent up to the room.

I was still a small-town kid from rural Canada, but even I knew that Dom Pérignon was a high-class act.

3. The Emerging Artist

Each summer, the Canadian Figure Skating Association conducts a national seminar, where the country's top skaters, and those with promising futures, spend a week working on training techniques with high-quality instructors.

In 1981, the seminar was held during the last week of August in London, Ontario, on the scenic grounds of the University of Western Ontario. We were billeted at a campus residence. There were about five dozen of us at the singles seminar — the ice-dance seminar had been held in June — including Tracey Wainman, Elizabeth Manley and fifteen-year-old Kurt Browning. This summer we dissected spinning technique under Dr. Hellmut May; sweated through painful off-ice conditioning with Carol Rossignol of the CFSA; and worked with dance master Andre Denis (who contributed to the success of Rob McCall and Tracy Wilson, our superb ice-dance team). Because of the success he'd had with Tracey Robertson and me — and Tracey Wainman had been skating with us all summer, too — Doug Leigh was one of the key instructors.

Heading up a choreography session was a vital, demonstrative, and very attractive German-American blonde who combined a love of music with a knowledge of skating, dance and theatrics. She talked about "energy flow," capturing an "inner feeling," and the recognition that underneath the sport of figure skating was the art form of figure skating. The main message was that if you encouraged this feeling, your programs would say something about you, and not be just a disjointed collection of tricks.

It was my first encounter with Uschi Keszler.

It had been six months since I won Canadians and the steady grind of preparing for a new season distanced us from the euphoria of that great spring. I was hearing and reading that I was merely a jumper, an unexpressive leaper who had no feel for music, no connecting steps, no sense of what I was trying to portray.

It was fair criticism. I had a terrible time interpreting music. The reputation I had as a non-artistic type was entirely accurate and it did have me worried a bit. But choreography was not high on my priority list and I didn't relish the idea of this session of the seminar.

I was more concerned with the tricks than I was with presentation. But in the slow portion of my freeskating program there were a couple of steps which, for some reason, I loved the feeling of. I remember I was stepping from backwards to forwards and I just sort of coasted on a forward edge and hopped into another step. It's a phrase I still have in my program. Out of the whole five minutes, there were only these two brief steps which made me feel a certain sensation, and I didn't even know why.

At the seminar, we had to do our long programs for Uschi, and those two steps immediately caught her eye. She recognized the kind of flow she had been talking to us about and

she suggested that I try to spread that flow through everything I did on the ice. She said, "Those two steps have the
flow. That's what it is. You've already got it . . . now do every
step in your program with that feeling."

Luckily I had something to relate to. I had those two steps
to take the feeling from or I might never have caught it. Before
you can get to the point of projecting yourself artistically, you
must first feel that sensation yourself. It's much more than
physical. Sometimes you watch a skater or a dance team and
you say "There's something about that guy" but you just
can't pinpoint it. They're completely in touch with the sensation of skating. Torvill and Dean have it; that's what's magical
about them. They weren't much more dramatic than anyone
else, but they had that edge, and it elevated them to a completely different plane. They don't even do any tricks when
they warm up. They just skate. But your eyes are riveted on
them because they have that feeling and you can sense it. I
went to Barbara Graham and said I wanted to work with
Uschi and some extra ice time was arranged. Unfortunately,
the only free time was at five o'clock on the Sunday morning,
our only day off. But figure skaters who train in the off-hours
at hockey rinks are used to that.

I worked hard at that morning session, and I think Uschi
was impressed by my dedication. She said later she liked how
I went at everything "a hundred-thousand times" until I got it
right.

I was just in awe of Uschi that week. We clicked. She
couldn't tell me enough. A bunch of us went out for dinner
and she and I talked right through the meal. We talked about
paying the price for excellence; about how you can't make a
person exciting, but you can make them comfortable and free;
about Uschi's theories on movement and motion. In Philadelphia, she had worked with a blind skater, Stosh Serafin.
Trying to improve her teaching, Uschi studied movement for
ten years with Dr. Marjorie Turner, a famous dance theorist

from Rutgers University. Uschi was not an opportunist, but she wanted to find someone to display her discoveries with. She's not into having a big name, money or anything like that. She just wanted to say something within the skating world and needed the right skater to act as a vehicle.

Doug was also taken with Uschi. Until that summer, Suzanne Russell had done our choreography on a part-time basis. She was moving into the city, though, and starting a family, and wasn't going to be able to work with me any more. I wasn't that worried: I just wanted to jump and spin and skate fast.

But meeting Uschi began to alter that. Since Doug, whose judgment I trust implicitly, was also impressed by her approach, it became apparent that she would start to work with us. I began to go to Mannheim with her for a two-week session every December, and it became one of my most demanding work periods. One of Doug's strongest points as a coach is that he's not jealous. If bringing someone else on board will help his skaters with a weakness, then he doesn't let ego or pride stand in the way, even if that person may be given some of the credit for success. So there was no question that Uschi would join us. Many, many top coaches aren't nearly as selfless.

With that seminar in London, I felt another one of those doors opening. Uschi taught me that while movement has a beginning and end, like moving your arm, *motion* is continuous; the new movement starts before the old one ends, and is pulled by a constant energy flow. Uschi helped me to discover that in an organized program, I could, and should, be pulled by the same free-flow sensation that I had loved when I flung myself onto the ice as a six-year-old, when I was swimming and diving, when I soared over a mogul at Mountainview or when I flipped out of a neckspring off that old leather footstool. I was still extremely shy, but Doug and Uschi knew that in the deepest part of my heart, I wanted to communicate the sensation to an audience of thousands. It became a matter of working hours and hours — years, really — to capture that sensation in every movement I made on the ice.

The London seminar was not the first occasion on which Uschi Keszler had watched Brian Orser. She had been at the 1981 Worlds in Hartford working with West German pair Christian Reigel and Andreas Nischwitz, who were surprise bronze-medallists.

"We had all heard about this young Canadian skater who was doing this triple axel and I couldn't wait to see him. I'm not sure he impressed me on the ice, because what I remember more is being in the same elevator with him at the hotel, and thinking to myself, 'So this is Brian Orser. He looks so preppy!' You know, with the glasses and clean-cut look. I remember hoping to myself that he wasn't boring. But when I met them in London, I immediately liked both him and Doug. I could tell right away that they were real people. They didn't have any of that phoniness that sometimes goes with figure skating. Maybe because they were small-town guys."

In another one of those recurring links to 1962, Keszler's appearance at the seminar had been arranged by Donald Jackson, an old acquaintance. Keszler was already working with Claudia Leistner of West Germany, whose career would peak with a silver medal at the 1982 Worlds, and was scheduled to go to New York to work with u.s. champion Elaine Zayak — the 1982 World Champion — but the dates conflicted with the CFSA seminar. In a decision that would influence Canadian skating history, she opted for the seminar.

As a choreographer, Keszler was still relatively unknown, but as a skater she had been a graceful sensation. Born in the west-central city of Mannheim, one of the two West German skating hotbeds (Oberstdorf is the other), Keszler started skating in 1954, at the age of six. Her first skates were actually a set of blades, five sizes too big, that bolted onto her street shoes. As Brian Orser followed his sister to the rink, so Uschi Keszler tagged after her older brother. Her father was a turbine engineer and her mother a full-time housewife. Their first child arrived ten years into their marriage, Uschi five years later. They were actually a skiing family, but one winter there was no snow, so Uschi's older brother took up skating and she followed suit. She showed promise, but also nurtured other interests as she grew up. She had been studying ballet, jazz and other dance forms since the age of three, became a school track-and-field champion, passed her gold-medal tests in roller skating (a sport from which many European ice skaters make a transition) and competed in ballroom-dance contests.

By 1961, she became German novice skating champion; in 1962, she won the junior title; and in 1965 she won the national senior championship to complete the same triple that Brian Orser would sweep in Canada. At seventeen, she finished tenth in that Worlds, which was won by Peggy Fleming.

Then disaster struck. Tuberculosis was prevalent in the family: her uncle had it; her grandmother died at the age of thirty-seven from TB. A haggard Keszler contracted the disease immediately after the 1966 Worlds. She spent eight lonely and frightening months in a sanatorium, gazing out the window at the Black Forest. "I came to appreciate life and real people during that time, and realized what passion I had for skating," she recalls. She returned to the ice, suffered a relapse and listened to a doctor tell her she could never skate again. Brian Orser would say that his World title in 1987 was for the championship Uschi never won.

She wrote to the United States Figure Skating Association, enquiring about coaching jobs. Instead of a coaching position, she received an offer to skate professionally with Ice Follies. "If the doctor hadn't said 'never, never' about my skating, I might not have done it, but I was determined to prove him wrong." She watched the 1967 Worlds as the Ice Follies' guest in Vienna, then joined the show, where she met the star — Donald Jackson.

On tour, she took up the roles left by retired Ena Bauer (after whom a skating move is named) and found herself playing Viking goddesses, the Queen of American Skating, and several other parts smacking of royalty. "As a child I always wanted to be a princess at Hallowe'en," she says with a laugh. "And never got to be. When I turned pro, that's all I got." At one show in San Francisco, the Viking goddess was carried onto the ice on a shield, a moment identified later by a five-year-old witness as the instant he decided he wanted to be a figure skater. That five-year-old was Brian Boitano, Brian's Orser's future rival.

Soon after joining the Follies, Keszler met Aram Boornazian, a rabid skating fan from Philadelphia, who at one time had been a member of the rock group The Elegants. He penned their hit "Little Star" and several other top-ten tunes of the 1950s. Remaining in the music business, he had built a chain of successful record stores in the east. They were married two weeks after they met and Uschi quit the show after just a year. Eleven months later, she gave birth to their only child, Marc, putting to rest another doctor's dire prediction that she would never have children.

Brian likes to surprise people by pointing out that Uschi has a son in university. She turns male heads with her Teutonic good looks and stunning figure, and is always draped in furs and diamonds. At first blush, the temptation is to dismiss her as a mere bombshell, and many have made this mistake. But Keszler is a highly motivated, intelligent woman with a piercing eye for a person's good and bad traits. Her intimate understanding of movement is often underrated in world figure-skating circles. In fact, she may be ahead of her time in teaching style. Like Doug Leigh, most of her thoughts and energies are directed toward figure skating.

She recalls that extra session at the summer seminar: "They were all there — Michelle, Marilyn Leigh, everybody — and when Doug took me there at 5:00 A.M., Brian was already skating. That impressed the hell out of me. At the very end of the session, he fell on his last jump, and smashed his hand down on the ice in great anger, and I said to myself, 'That kid has it.' I could see that he had the total scope of emotions, the high and the low, and it was just a matter of developing them. I knew right then I wanted to work at it."

Keszler joined the Orser team that fall. While there has never been any doubt that Doug Leigh ultimately calls the shots, they work well in tandem. Doug has been the technical genius, and Uschi the artistic mentor, but there is always an overlap in their duties. Just as there is in the two sets of figure-skating marks, which Doug and Uschi personify.

Keszler also remembers even the most minute slight. Butch Orser was a little suspicious of her when she joined the Orser team. Costs were beginning to mount — Brian and Doug had also added Karol Divin as a coach for compulsory figures. At a competition in Montreal, Uschi was telling Butch that Brian needed to develop certain artistic talents, which lay hidden inside of him, and Butch turned quickly and snapped, "And what do you do?"

Five years later in Cincinnati, after a spectacular short program by Brian which left the audience gasping, Butch, who had long since become an Uschi booster, said, "Normally in a short program you're aware of the seven elements and you're counting them. But we were a minute and a half into the program and I realized I hadn't consciously counted any elements yet."

Uschi Keszler turned slowly to Butch Orser and smiled. "That," she said, "is what I do."

It was at the seminar in London that I realized that being champion was not all glory, cozy sentiment and the chills of victory. Now, everyone had their hands in it, trying to help me out. They all wanted a piece of me. People were full of advice, saying, "Do this, do that," and I guess I cracked a little.

At one session, I kicked the boards out of anger and cried. Michelle drove me back to the room where I continued to cry. In retrospect, it was the reaction of a small-town boy thrust suddenly into the national spotlight. All eyes were on me, everyone wanted to be part of it and I had to live up to people's expectations every minute. What transpired was a bit of a mental breakdown. I didn't know what was happening to me, and I was scared.

Over the following few days I started to learn to live with the stress of being a champion, although the pressure continued occasionally to affect me. I was, after all, only nineteen. A few months previously I had been skating alone in cold, dark rinks, where hardly anyone but Doug and the maintenance man knew what I was up to.

That fall the ISU decided to shorten the freeskate program from five to four and a half minutes in an effort to cut down the number of big tricks, and increase the artistry in skating. Their reasoning was that if you spent twenty-five seconds setting up for two triple Lutzes, you wouldn't have much time for anything else, and would be hurting your chances of high marks.

An American choreographer, Ruben Huron, had helped put my music together — Uschi hadn't joined us yet — and when we timed the program, we discovered that somehow the three of us had made a mistake. It was nearly a minute short. In skating the program, I thought it seemed to take far less time to complete than in the past, but assumed the difference was just the thirty seconds that the ISU had lopped off.

My first fall international that season was in England, at the prestigious St. Ivel competition, in the London suburb of Richmond. The first thing you do at a competition is take a cassette of your music to the music director, who tests it out on the rink's public-address system. Shortly after I did that, I got a call at my hotel saying that somehow my program was at least forty seconds too short. No wonder it had seemed so quick.

We felt like a couple of rookies. During practice sessions

before St. Ivel, Doug and I took the slow portion of the program, repeated it, added a couple of moves and inserted them later in the program. After a couple of days, it was ready to skate. In that embryonic stage of our international experience we were able to do that. In later years, every second, every *half*-second was accounted for weeks in advance, and I couldn't have changed a single movement without upsetting the exact timing and rhythm of the show. That precision was an outgrowth of what we learned from the terrible mistake before the 1981 St. Ivel event.

I was second in figures, won the short, and the patchwork program was good enough to win the long over David Santee, who had been second in the world that spring in Hartford.

My reputation was still founded upon the triple axels, but all that summer I had been forced to omit them during practices because of severe stress fractures in my left leg.

The axel puts tremendous pressure on the takeoff leg and exerts immense torque on the landing leg. That often results in injuries. The stress fracture really bothered me when I did the axel, so I had to forgo it during summer school.

The axel was back for my second fall competition, Skate Canada, in the last weekend of October in Ottawa. Norbert Schramm was considered to be the one to beat. When he won the figures and I was fourth, the gold was his. He did a great job on the crowd with his flashy short and long programs, but I won both those events to take the silver. It was the best I had ever skated to that point. An indication of how we were progressing with the non-technical portions of skating were my first two 5.9s in artistic merit. With lots of off-ice stretching and training, and Uschi's dance classes and theories, I was becoming more flexible and interpretive.

The next day, I flew to Toronto with Gordon Forbes and Ghislain Briand, who by now was training in Orillia. I was using my mother's eleven-year-old Thunderbird, a classic car, for transportation and we had left it at the Toronto airport. All of us were fatigued from the weekend. After dropping Gordon off at his Toronto apartment, I asked Ghislain if he would mind driving. I drifted off to sleep in the front seat.

That evening, the telephone rang at Doug Leigh's Orillia home. On the other end of the line was skating coach Greg Myles, who quickly relayed some disturbing news.

The 1971 Thunderbird with Brian and Ghislain on board had gone out of control a few hours earlier on a downgrade of Highway 400, about twenty-five miles north of Toronto. The driver had nodded off. The car had swung right and careened into guard rails, some of which had sliced into the metal, forcing the car to flip over. It had continued to bounce off the guard rails on its roof before landing in a ditch. Brian was staying with Greg and his wife Judy in Orillia, and Greg had taken the call from the hospital.

"I nearly had a heart attack," Leigh recalls. "I could picture the two of them lying in pieces."

But Greg told him that Brian had miraculously escaped with only a few stitches in one knee, and that Ghislain's main wound was to his psyche. He was filled with remorse. During the terrifying moments when he opened his eyes to find the car sailing through the air he was so worried about his friend that all he could do was scream, "Brian, Brian, Brian."

I suppose that when Ghislain called my name I woke up. I had fallen asleep without a seat belt on, which may have saved my life. The passenger side of the car was completely crushed, so that the inside of the roof was touching the seat. But the motion of the flipping car tossed me over to the other side and, despite a severe scare, I was all right. The car was totalled though.

I knew there would be no problem with my parents, they would just be concerned about our safety, and I was right. Ghislain felt terrible, but my parents didn't blame him. He didn't fall asleep on purpose. We were safe and the incident was quickly forgotten. Ghislain is still a friend. A few years later I stood as best man at his wedding.

I got back on the ice and started working toward the national championships, which were to be held in Brandon, Manitoba.

There had been a lot of talk about Brian Pockar regaining his title. He won the figures, while I was third. I won the short program and he skated poorly, and was fourth, so with the still-new marking system, we were tied with 2.2 placing points each.

In the long program, I didn't perform as well as I could. I was feeling the pressure of defending the title for the first time. It only really affected me at Canadians. The rest of the year, before and after, I skated well.

I landed the axel, but put my hand down on the Lutz and I was quite tired, so the ending was very weak. Tracey Wainman had spent the year with us in Orillia and she had a terrible time trying to defend her title. She got sick, put on a dismal performance and didn't even make the World team. Back then, it was hard for Doug and me to face the reality of something not working right. We worked a thousand times on every move. A competitive performance was supposed to be merely the thousand-and-first repetition. We were still acquiring the knowledge of what it takes to perform at the highest level. Fortunately, we had plenty of time to learn — we were a year ahead of where Doug thought we should be. He had planned on 1982 as the year we made the World team. How to resist undue pressure in defending a title — Doug said, "We were better as the hunter than the hunted," — was just another thing we had to learn.

I didn't know if I had won, but thank goodness, I had the right panel. I won five judges, two of them on tie-breakers when I had one point more for technical merit than Brian did.

Everyone was thrilled, because Brian had skated well. Many thought he had beaten me, but he made some mistakes, too. It could have gone either way. It probably didn't hurt that Canada's future was pegged on me, since I was still developing and had done well at the previous Worlds.

Worlds that year were in Copenhagen and I had a dismal start. I finished twelfth in figures. This was a drastic improvement when you consider that I was *seventeenth* on the first figure. Jozef Sabovcik was eighteenth on that figure. I was very nervous. I think everything had happened too quickly for me and I just wasn't there.

That twelfth got me into the second-last group for short program, and I drew the first position, so I was skating sixteenth from the end. My combination was the double flip-triple toe and that was to be the final year for that combination. The way the flip takes off, you have to do it first, which leaves only triple toe or triple loop. The ISU took the flip out of compulsory combinations because in 1982 the skaters were going down like ten-pins. Igor Bobrin, David Santee, Fumio Igarashi all tumbled on the combination. That shows you how much skating has progressed. For someone not to be able to do a triple toe after a double flip now would be unthinkable. They're doing it in junior competition.

Only Scott Hamilton, Brian Pockar and I did the combination cleanly. Although I skated sixteenth from the end, I was in first place in the short program until the final two skaters, Hamilton and Schramm, who finished one-two. I was third and Brian Pockar fifth. Brian had had trouble in practice all week with the combination, but got tough and dug it out in the program.

Former World pairs champion Frances Dafoe started designing my costumes that year, and Margaret Sandor actually made them. They worked on CBC-TV productions and the Charlottetown Festival. They were very good, and I loved my costumes — all except that first one, which was a heavy blue Spandex. It contributed to the fatigue I felt in the long program.

I was scheduled to skate first in the final group. In my inexperience, I tore around through the full warm-up period, almost until they called my name. So, I started the program tired. (The next season, during fall sessions, Doug and I would simulate drawing every position in the skating order for the long program and practice the warm-up for it. If I skated first or second, I'd come off early to get ready.)

I went out and just died. I did a great triple axel, but put my hand down on my triple Lutz. I did a double toe instead of a triple, and opened up a Salchow. I still finished third in the long, behind Hamilton and Schramm, who took gold and silver, respectively.

The bronze went to Brian Pockar, who skated as well as, if not better than, he had ever skated in his life. He put together consistent short and long programs, finished fourth in the long, and that was enough to move him into third. In effect, my finishing third in the long paved the way for him to win the bronze under the new scoring system, which finally came around to helping him.

I think Brian would probably agree that I helped his skating by giving him incentive and motivation to work harder. The same thing holds for me with my chief rivals. Even though I didn't win gold at the Olympics, I felt I was a better skater than I'd ever been because I felt I had to match or better the work Brian Boitano had been doing with Canadian choreographer Sandra Bezic.

The ISU also gives separate medals for figures and freestyle. I took the bronze for freeskating. Brian Pockar's bronze medal was the first World medal for Canada in nine years, the first since Toller Cranston's bronze. It was a major breakthrough, and gave the Canadian team a psychological lift. We would add many more over the rest of the decade.

Still green, I didn't know that the ISU had a European tour. I had made commitments to appear in a number of carnivals in small towns back home, including Midland, so when I was asked to go on tour, which included the Soviet Union, I had to say no.

Brian Pockar retired soon after the Worlds to go into broadcasting and professional skating. On the night before the ISU tour, he and I sat in a hotel room and talked for much of the night about our careers and having been rivals and friends. We both left with good feelings.

The way I looked at it, I left Copenhagen in fourth place, two places better than the year before. I hadn't skated my very best, but I was still fourth in the world. And ever since the talk that night, I've had complete trust in Brian Pockar.

Heading into the 1983 season, there was a competition in Kitchener, Ontario, that would foreshadow a far more publicized confrontation on the same Hallowe'en weekend five years later.

When Brian Boitano and I met at Skate Canada on the last weekend of October 1982, it was not yet the widely anticipated spectacle sports fans would relish at Calgary for Skate Canada in 1987 or the Olympics four months later. However, the labels and the hype were already in evidence, a minuscule preview of what we could expect later in the decade.

This Skate Canada wasn't billed as the "Battle of the Brians," but rather the "Battle of the Triple Axels." An American TV station did a split-screen comparison — "Who had the better triple axel?" — and showed Brian and me side-by-side going through our axels. Brian and I found it pretty amusing, because skating had never really had this kind of head-to-head comparative exposure on a sports newscast. I think it brought a lot of mainstream attention to the sport, and that had to help everybody, even if the axels were only one part of skating. I had been virtually alone with the triple axel since

1979. Now Brian was doing one, a good one, too, considering how tall (5-11 to my 5-7) he was. By the 1983 World championships, four skaters — myself, Thomas Hlavik, Boitano and Jozef Sabovcik — landed triple axels. "It's just like hidden windshield wipers on cars," Doug cracked to a reporter. "Somebody develops one and pretty soon all the cars have to have them." By 1986, the top skaters were able to do the axel in combination with the required jump in the short program.

I didn't win that Skate Canada in Kitchener, but not because of the triple axel. In fact, I won both the short and long, and landed the axel, but again a dismal figures result (I placed fifth) kept me away from the gold medal. I took the silver; Brian won the gold.

Earlier, I had taken on my chief rival of that year, Norbert Schramm, at St. Ivel. By then he was a superstar. He was European champion and enormously popular in his native West Germany, and all over the continent. He wasn't training well, and he was technically off in many of his jumps, but he could still deliver a good program in competition. He had the ability to rise to the occasion, especially with his showmanship.

But I won the gold medal there for the second year in a row, skating a very strong short and long program. My short was skated to the music from "Fame," the first of my "theme" programs, and I loved doing it.

At the nationals, I got my first perfect 6.0 mark at Montreal's Maurice Richard Arena. It came in the long program when I did the axel, Lutz and all the rest, including the first triple flip (a jump we'd hear about in the 1988 Olympics) I'd ever done in competition. I felt like I was just sailing through the program, playing to the audience. Someone wrote later, "You could see the fire in his eyes." I could feel it.

At the World championships in Helsinki, figures again found me at the bottom of a mountain looking up. I was eighth in the first and third figures and a disastrous twelfth in the middle figure. I finished eighth, still four better than the previous year, but a long way from the medals.

After the awful second figure, I was already feeling down when David Dore came up, and angrily snapped at me something about letting everyone down. I was devastated.

It is impossible to discuss the second golden age of Canadian skating without reflecting upon David Dore.

Dore can get emotional when he speaks of skating, what the sport has done for him, and its spectacular progress in Canada since the mid-seventies. He originally discovered skating as regenerative therapy after a childhood battle with polio. His gait still shows the effects of the disease. It is tempting to dismiss his skating career as undistinguished, but he passed his gold tests, which he once called his "personal Olympics." He turned to the organizational side of the sport and by 1972 he had been elected a director of the CFSA. He was also a respected competition judge. By 1976 he had become technical vice-president, chairing the powerful Skaters Development Committee, from which a great deal of CFSA policy emanated. It was he who presided over Brian Orser's Vienna Cup trial in 1979. In 1980, when he was thirty-nine years old, David Dore ascended to the association presidency.

The presidency, like most skating jobs, is a volunteer position, and Dore retained his post as a history teacher in a Toronto high school. Midway through his presidency, he left teaching to take a more lucrative position as executive-director of the Canadian Jewellers Association. His four-year term as president ended in the summer of 1984, but in July 1985, he was hired as the CFSA's full-time program coordinator. Six months later he was appointed to the new position of director general. Although, technically, he can be fired by the volunteer executive board, his power within the organization is considerable.

While Dore is a strong and occasionally abrasive personality, his strengths and accomplishments far outweigh his weaknesses. It is clear that Dore has been the right man at the right time for Canadian skating. The national program was in a shambles in the mid-seventies and there were few apparent successors to Karen Magnussen, Toller Cranston and Ron Shaver. Dore knew that it was too late to salvage the 1980 Olympics, so he focused on 1984 and 1988. As support money began to flow into the CFSA, Dore emphasized that the association was determined to capture international success. Finishing in the medals became a priority.

Skaters would be supported psychologically and financially, he said, if they did their jobs and met the CFSA demands. It was a necessary approach, first crystallized in the person of twelve-year-old Tracey Wainman who, despite placing third at the 1980 nationals, was selected for Worlds ahead of champion Heather Kemkaran and runner-up Janet Morrisey, neither of whom were viewed as future contenders. Although this cultivation of Wainman was eventually abandoned when her ability and desire reached a plateau, it sent a strong message to the skating community.

And the message was heard. After Toller Cranston won a bronze medal at the 1974 World championships (he was also third in the 1976 Olympics), Canada went nine years without winning a medal in any world event before Brian Pockar ended the drought with a bronze. That initiated a seven-year period during which Canada won two World championships, five World silver medals, and eight bronze medals, plus three Olympic silvers and an Olympic bronze. In 1979, Canada's World results were so poor that it could send only the minimum number of six skaters to the 1980 World championships. By 1986, Canada had a seventeen-skater team, the biggest in the world, and just one below the maximum. It was the fulfillment of a promise Dore had made upon becoming president. He also vowed to keep elite skaters in the sport longer, through special financing, another successful undertaking. He predicted the CFSA would develop better coaching, which it did, and would demand some return from the athletes after their amateur career. In 1987, he sent letters to the top skaters, providing them with an accounting of how much the CFSA had spent on them and pointedly asking what the skaters planned to do in gratitude after they turned pro.

Although former executive director Lou Lefaive was the mover and shaker, along with Chris Lang Associates, behind an innovative deal with CTV which brought the CFSA the best television deal in Canadian amateur sports, Dore set the philosophical tone of the agreement. He quickly became the official spokesman on Canadian skating matters.

There are many other helpful people — including a local-club volunteer base of thousands — and powerful veterans in the CFSA such as ISU representative Donald Gilchrist, Bob Howard, Joyce Hisey, and technical director Barbara Graham, but it is David Dore who is viewed, both at home and abroad, as the spearhead of Canadian success.

Brian Orser and pairs champions Barbara Underhill and Paul Martini were his special projects. He unabashedly cried when Underhill and Martini, the final pair to skate at Helsinki in 1983, appeared to have won the gold medal with a brilliant performance. His tears of joy turned to tears of rage when they were placed third.

Dore's career is most closely intertwined with that of Orser. In Dore's first year as technical vice-president, Orser won the novice championship. He was put on the fast track and, although he resisted attempts to move him to Toronto, he was fully supported in his international endeavors. He brought the CFSA money through exhibitions and was the first skater to be allowed a personal trust fund. Relations between Dore and the Orser camp — the skater, his family, Doug Leigh, Uschi Keszler — have run a gamut of contrasting emotions, but in general, especially over the final years of his career, Dore took significant steps to forward and *protect Brian's interests. After stepping down as president in 1984, an emotional Dore presented Brian with his coveted president's pin as thanks for the thrill of the silver-medal performance.*

What I eventually learned about David is that, when it comes to a disappointment, he has to get things off his chest. I don't know if it was because of his outburst or not, but I did skate a fine third figure on the loop, which pulled me back up into eighth. The loop is one of my better figures anyway, perhaps because the circles are tighter, and I have better control. In any case, the figures were over and so was the encounter with David.

The "Fame" program went off well. The required combination in the jump was a double toe loop and I did it first, followed by a triple toe. That turned into a big controversy. Some people said that I should have done a triple Lutz, a harder triple, followed by the double toe. Doug and I argued that it was harder doing the triple jump second, because you don't have the speed and momentum heading into the triple. I finished second in the short. Probably, had I done the Lutz instead, I would have won it, but that's hindsight. We had been practicing that combination since the summer.

The long was solid, although I had a minor problem with the axel, taking an extra crosscut going in and doing a little turn coming out, but the jump still counted. I was second in the long — including one 5.9 for artistic impression — which gave me an ISU silver medal in the freeskate, but only a bronze medal over all. Scott won with a strong performance, and Norbert was third in freeskating, which gave him the silver medal.

I was thrilled about winning my first World medal, but I can honestly say that it should have been a silver. Norbert did not skate well: the judges propped him up when there were others besides Scott and myself who should have beaten him in freeskating. Sometimes a skater will be propped up one

left: Brian wearing the captain's sweater of the Midland Novices. His hockey career short-lived.

right: The day Donald Jackson (shown here with Brian and Mary Kay) appeared in the ◄land Carnival was a turning point in Brian's career.

◄*ve:* Twelve-year-old Michelle Simpson and thirteen-year-old Brian Orser in the Elmvale ◄ival.

t: On the podium, after winning the 1981 Canadian National Championship, Brian was ?rcome with emotion.

ove: The World Championships were held in Ottawa in 1984. Brian placed second behind American, Scott Hamilton.

Top: Brian with Katarina Witt on the River Thames. Across the river is the legendary Richmond Rink, where Brian won a record three St. Ivel championships.

Above: David Dore (right of photographer) carved a career as a Canadian skating administrator and changed the face of Canadian skating. He is shown here with coach Dou Leigh and Brian at the Worlds in Cincinnati.

CFS

Right: Governor-General Jeanne Sauvé welcomes Brian to the Order of Canada in Ottawa i 1986.

Above: I did it! Coach Doug Leigh (left) and journalist Steve Milton (right) were together wi**t** Brian watching the television monitor as the results of the 1987 World Championships appeared.

MIKE DOD**▶**

Right: Finally – the top step of the podium: Cincinnati, 1987

CANADA WID**▶**

Left: At a reception in Orill Brian presented fourteen miniature gold medals to his coaches and members of his family. Here, Doug Leigh receives his.

Below: Sports Minister Otto Jelinek and Prime Minister Brian Mulroney were prese in Calgary when the annou cement was made that Bria would be Canada's Olymp: flag bearer.

Right: Brian's proudest moment as a Canadian.
PAUL WODEHOU!
CANADA W

Top: Final advice: choreographer Uschi Keszler and Brian confer during the last practice before the Olympic freeskate.

FRED THORNHILL/CANADA WIDE

Above: In Calgary with Brian were two key members of his team: Dr. Peter Jensen (left) and Doug Leigh (right).

FRED THORNHILL/CANADA WIDE

Right: On the podium in Calgary, from left to right: Brian, Brian Boitano, and Victor Petrenko.

IAN TOMLINSON

Left: Canada's top two Olympians in 1988 are also longtime friends. Liz Manley and Brian Orser celebrate their silver medals.

FRED THORNHILL/
CANADA WIDE

Brian's first world team (right) and his last (below). David Dore's dream was to increase the size of the team and to raise its profile. Obviously, he succeeded.

op left: It all came down to the long program: four years of preparation ended in four and a *al*f minutes of skating. IAN TOMLINSON

eft: Brian's second career – as a partner in a pair of Cultures restaurants franchises – now *a*bsorbs an increasing amount of his time. IAN MACDONALD/CANADA WIDE

Above: Brian with his mother and father. JIM WILEY

Overleaf: Thanking the crowd at the 1986 Canadian Championships. Brian wore the same *H*ungarian costume in his final exhibition at the Worlds in Budapest, when he skated to the *H*ungarian Rhapsody Number Six.

year, but if he continues not to deliver, he will get the marks he deserves the next. This happened to Norbert in 1984.

It was my first time on the World podium. When they raised the Maple Leaf up the flagpole, I was thrilled. I remember turning to Scott and saying, "I *like* this." I knew then that I would never allow myself to miss being on the podium again.

On the final Sunday of a World championship, there is always an exhibition in the city that has played host to the event. It is a good time for the skaters, a chance to wash out the taste of tense competition, and skate free-form. The audience loves it. It's almost always the first program sold out.

I had been working on a program that was a radical departure for me. It was Uschi's idea to skate to the music from *The Pink Panther*. We started working on it in Orillia before the World championships. I was opposed, fearful that it wouldn't work. I was still shy, and still not fully committed to taking artistic chances.

The program had me finishing prone on the ice, in a smiling, mocking pose, as if I were that Pink Panther cartoon figure from the Peter Sellers movies. The show was full of humorous, cat-like movements and saucy gestures at the crowd. Uschi had done a marvelous job in designing it, but she really had to work to get me to agree to it.

Then I got the costume from Mrs. Sandor. It was completely black except for a pink belt, pink gloves, pink boots and a pink bowtie. In Helsinki, I was somewhat embarrassed putting the costume on, still unconvinced that this kind of showmanship was for me. When I stepped on the ice, a low, puzzled murmur went through the audience. Hearing it increased my apprehension.

Then the music started, and they all started to cheer and laugh and clap. I was thinking "Wow! This is the easiest ovation I ever had." I always thought I had to do the triple axel, but I felt this work. People came up to me later, telling me how much they enjoyed it, and with that program — one single two-minute show, thousands of miles from home — things changed for me. I was pulled out of myself. I was no longer shy about letting go and expressing myself on the ice.

Barb and Paul had also won a bronze medal — David Dore was not alone in thinking that it should have been a gold — and we all took part in both the European and North American ISU tours. We all had a great time.

In the spring of 1983, I began showing a quadruple toe loop in practice. It was a bit of smokescreen, as I had only a small intention of ever including it in competition, and then only if it was very consistent. It was meant to keep my competition guessing and to let the ISU know that I was working on new things. I wanted to keep them talking and I did. The press really took hold of it, although one or two knew I'd probably never put one in my program. Increasingly, however, I was turning away from technical feats to focus on the artistry.

On the U.S. tour, Tom Collins took everyone in the cast to the musical that was tearing up Broadway in 1983. As we watched *Cats* I was very motivated by the movement and the music. I liked the cat-like motions and it was in sync with what I was doing already in Helsinki. I took the idea back to Orillia that something from *Cats* would be the music for my short program the next year — the Olympic year of 1984.

It had been an exciting year — a gold at St. Ivel, my first World medal, my first 6.0 mark, the reception to my exhibition program, and now the idea for a new program. That spring, Scott, Jozef and I made a three-cornered vow that, when they gave out the medals at the Olympics, it would be the three of us on the podium.

I'm not convinced there is any consecutive five minutes in sport as lonely as a competitive figure-skating program. Perhaps a pitcher in the bottom of the ninth inning of a World

Series game with the bases loaded can experience the same sense of isolation, or maybe a high jumper in his third attempt at a particular height, or a goaltender facing a penalty shot. These are all major athletic crises, indeed, but they are quickly resolved. A figure skater's sense of being abandoned to his own ability, without teammates, without competitors, without coaches out there with him, lasts much longer. A singles skater's pursuit is, by its very nature, a solitary one.

It is important that a skater's self-assurance be stoked by confidence not only in his own abilities, but also in those of his coach and choreographer. I have had complete faith in Doug and Uschi, but I've been fortified by another source as well: my family.

Our strong family ties have played a significant role in any success I've enjoyed. A sense of family can nurture a strong sense of self-worth, and I think all five of us have benefited from that, thanks to diligent work by our parents. Over the final years of my amateur career, it became very important to me that all the members of my family — and their husbands and wives — be around at a major competition. I gather strength from them, appreciate what each has to offer and maybe what I, in turn, can offer them.

A child who attempts to achieve a lofty goal, such as becoming the world's best, not just in skating but in any discipline, puts pitfalls in the path of any parents. We've all heard horror stories about stage mothers and hockey fathers. I've seen similar destruction caused by parents too anxious to push a talented skater who consequently ignore their other children. There wasn't any of that in our family. Certainly, figure skating has been a huge part of our lives, and all the kids know the sport extremely well. They're interested in how their "baby" brother does.

But in our family, there's always been an awareness that each person is different, that each of the kids would do his or her own thing. My thing was skating. Period. We definitely recognize one another's gifts in life and we generally don't compete against one another. There was some slight competition between Mary Kay and me, when we were young, because we were in the same sport. I think there might be some bit of envy, but my brothers and sisters aren't jealous of me.

I'm very envious of Janice, because she had the determination and the intelligence to stick with school, going away each fall and winter to earn her degree at the University of Guelph. Janice is the brains of the family and we all knew that she had the smarts. I was very proud of her and used to brag a lot about her at school because she studied her brains out every night and got AS in everything.

If you ever had a problem, especially a financial one, you talked to Janice. She used to do my bank book. She would try, time after time, to get me to balance, or at least to write down what I was spending. Of course, I wouldn't. If I was five cents off, she'd be in there fighting for the five cents. And that's for all of us. Janice doesn't differ from one brother to the other. She's the great organizer in our family. Over the past four or five years I've become really close to Janice. She and I always got along because she seemed to understand me the best when I was a kid. She was the big sister, and I loved doing things for her. Being the youngest has been great. I got away with a lot of things. But Janice was the oldest and had to set an example. She set a fine example for all of us. I saw how she applied herself and I got some of my work habits, which I think are good, from her.

In the past six or seven years I've also got to know my brother Bob, who's the second oldest. Bob's main strength is his incredible ability to turn a negative thing around and make something positive out of it. When we were growing up, he had long hair and was something of a rebel. He had different priorities, which were accepted, but I felt that I didn't know him too well. He used to play the drums and had a band, Blue Dust, which jammed in the basement of our house in Penetang. For a long time he was an outsider in the family. He used to come in, go downstairs to his bedroom, lock the door and come out only for dinner. It was a period he went through, but he turned it all around, and we all got to know him. He gained a great deal of confidence as life went along. In the mid-eighties he went to Greece on a project for Coke International, and did a superb job. He's also a really good racquetball player. He's very quiet and he's very proud. He also brags about me all the time. I know because people tell me about it.

My other brother, Michael, is the comedian in the family. He injects humor into any situation, good or bad, and he can get away with it. He's a regular guy. He doesn't have any ego problems whatsoever, and he doesn't have to rub shoulders with the right people in society. In fact, he has a bit of a wild streak, and has always liked a good time.

I actually think Michael was too smart for school. Like Janice, he has a very high IQ, but he never applied himself at school. But he picks up on all kinds of things a lot quicker than I can. He's also a handyman. He built an addition on his house. When I didn't win in Geneva in 1986, things looked awfully bleak, but somehow he found some humor in it. Whenever there are key decisions to be made, or there is a bad development, we have a family meeting. Like any family, we have had some sad times, but Michael will crack a funny at the right time, just when we need it, to loosen things up.

Just as Michael can lighten a situation, Mary Kay seems to be able find the right thing to say at the right time. She has a way with words that the rest of us don't quite have. For instance, six weeks before the Calgary Olympics, I'd had a really bad day and the magnitude of what lay ahead of me really came down heavy on me. When I got home, there was a card from Mary Kay that read, "If you take a lump of coal and add a lot of pressure, it turns into a diamond." It was exactly what I needed.

I turn to her for that kind of thing. She knows what to do, partly because we are so close in age, partly because we skated together from the beginning, right until I was sixteen. We competed against each other to acquire new skills. I probably competed more strongly because I was younger. I got my axel first; she got her double Salchow first; she got her dance first. She had a few moments when she really shone, for example, when she won the summer competition in Ottawa.

Mary Kay was the one who had to deal most with the attention I got, because she was skating, too. I think her leaving the amateur ranks to turn pro with Ice Follies helped her deal with it. It was one of the best things she ever did. Although Janice went away to school, Mary Kay was the first to go that far away for a full year. We went down to Toledo and Columbus the year I first won senior Canadians to see her skate, because Follies didn't come to Canada. We were all so proud of her.

My skating was absorbed into the family and became another factor, albeit a significant one, in our lifestyle. My parents worked hard, I guess we all did, at the difficult task of making sure that skating didn't completely disrupt family life. Part of the reason I moved to Orillia when I was sixteen was that my parents didn't want to see the whole household revolve around my skating. I've been fortunate in having parents who were able to balance everyone else's needs, while at the same time standing with me all the way through skating.

And fortunate in having parents who could afford it.

It is no secret that figure skating is a very expensive sport. There comes a point, as it did for me when I began to take lessons from Doug, when you have to decide whether you're serious about the sport. Then it becomes a financial drain.

There have been skaters whose families have had to make huge sacrifices for the sport, and others who have had to drop out when it got too expensive. That's especially true in the United States, where they don't have the financial support from their association and government that Canadians have enjoyed since the mid-seventies. Still, I know of one of our top skaters who once had to hock a medal just to buy some dress clothes.

By the time I was ten years old, my parents were spending at least $2,000 a year (in 1971 dollars, too) on my skating, and they also had Mary Kay to provide for. I had to register in skating schools. Then I took private lessons from Doug, and I was also taking dance lessons from Tom Harrison and engaging in off-ice training. I was boarded during summer school. There was also the expense of the gas for the incessant driving from rink to rink, and the cost of competition costumes and new skates.

My dad claims my skating never cost him more than $12,000 a year, but I think he is overlooking a number of things. Among other things, once I started travelling out of the country for major competitions, my parents wanted to make sure that Doug was there, too, so they paid his way if he wasn't a designated team coach.

Until I moved to Orillia, my parents in effect maintained two homes during the summer, buying a trailer and parking it at Tudhope Park on Lake Couchiching so my mom could stay there while Mary Kay and I were at summer school. Whenever there was a competition, my parents would be there. They had to take a hotel room, pay for food, parking and all the incidental costs of travel. As time went on, all my brothers and sisters, and their spouses came, too. My parents' room soon became the unofficial team headquarters. There was always a party there, paid for by my parents, after my long program. That continued right through my final competition. There were always plenty of CFSA people, friends from home who happened to attend the event, and even some media.

All of this cost significantly more than the $10,000 to

$12,000 a year my dad will admit to, but my parents spent it willingly.

We received some help. As I moved up the ranks, I also began collecting more money from Sport Canada. In 1981, I became an A-card athlete, qualifying for living expenses. The CFSA's elite skater program helped with training and travel, first through the Skaters Development Fund, then through the Best Ever Committee and, by 1982, the Athlete's Trust fund for the World team. Eventually, the CFSA required a budget from Doug and me, in which we listed what we felt was necessary for the year. That started off as a training budget: Doug was required to submit a plan of how I was going to train each year. It was later broadened to include finances. The CFSA would then decide how much they could chip in, and my parents would pay the rest. In 1984 my dad played a little hardball with the association, and I became the first Canadian skater to have my trust fund, just like skiers have had for years, and that generated more income for my training. My dad insisted that the other World team members have the same advantage. It worked to the benefit of the CFSA , in the end: they received a bigger cut than the ski association got from their athletes' endorsements and performance fees.

It was much cheaper to live in Orillia than in any of the big skating centers. Doug's lessons were cheaper; ice time was cheaper; and accommodations were enormously cheaper. When other national-team members were paying $700 to $800 a month for rent in Toronto, we bought a townhouse near Twin Lakes Arena for $40,000. And I got some breaks, especially when I trained part time at Toronto's Cricket Club, and wasn't charged ice rental.

Despite all of this, my parents still had to make sacrifices, especially in the early years. They didn't join clubs, go out, or spend money on themselves. Their philosophy was that when money was needed they went out to get it. People might forget that they didn't actually own the Coke plant until 1979, and that my dad only came to Penetang on the understanding that he could buy stock based on performance bonuses.

My dad is a self-made man by the strictest definition of the term. When he came out of the armed forces, he went to work for Coca-Cola. He drove delivery trucks in Windsor. He met my mom when they both came to the hospital to visit a mutual friend who had broken his neck. After eight years, my dad was made a sales supervisor. As his family began to grow, and Janice took up skating in Windsor, he looked for ways to make extra money. He talked my grandfather into opening a coin laundry when that industry was in its infancy, and it did well. He sold it for a profit when we moved to Belleville. Then he took the job in Penetang because it might eventually be parlayed into ownership. At the same time, he ran at least one business on the side, always in a partnership. For five years, my parents owned a store in Midland called the Corner Cupboard, close to the house and the rink. Janice ran a shift there when she was thirteen, collecting $5 a day. We all worked there, including me when I had time after skating. My parents also owned three different vending companies and held the cafeteria contract at the mammoth RCA plant in Midland for years. They used the commissary facilities to put together the supplies for the vending machines.

My dad took some chances and risks in the business world in order to provide for us. He probably made some mistakes that I don't even know about. I've felt fortunate that my parents have been able to afford the best things for us, but I've never felt guilty, and my parents never made me, or let me feel guilty. What they did was make opportunities for us. They never handed things to us. If we had to pay money for the opportunity, it was still up to us to make something out of it. Like the skating — they can't go out and do it for me, no matter how much they pay. I later had that attitude reconfirmed in the business world when I got into Cultures Restaurants franchises. Everyone is offered an opportunity once in a while; it's what you do with it that make the difference. From my parents I learned to take an opportunity and run with it.

When I'm asked who my idol is in skating, I don't talk about Toller Cranston or Donald Jackson. I say my dad. I've seen what he's done with his business and his family, how he's handled himself in situations, jubilant ones and depressing ones. He never told us what to do, but he pointed the way and then let us settle things on our own.

There isn't a day when I'm talking to my dad that he doesn't say he loves me. Ever since we were little, our family has done that. My parents, especially my dad, are physical. That slogan, "Have you hugged your child today?" I think my parents started it.

My dad says things, my mom shows things. She is emotional. She cries a lot — we've all seen that. She's so concerned for her children. When I won junior in Thunder Bay, she watched the short program but couldn't take it. She didn't watch the long. I won, and since then she hasn't watched a program, other than 1982. She always goes out into the corridor for a cigarette. She's become superstitious about it now. The television networks made a big deal about it in 1988, following her around the Saddledome.

Both my parents, considering that they have money, lack pretension. My mom goes out and plays bingo in Penetang for three hours every week. She would do anything for her kids. She did all that driving in the early days when we travelled from rink to rink for practices. The Orillia-Barrie-Midland triangle is in one of the worst snowbelts in Canada, and there was rarely a winter day that we didn't encounter treacherous conditions somewhere on the highway. My mom didn't complain. If the road wasn't closed, we always made it. She never said, "You know, kids, maybe you should stay home this time." When I came home from school and got the skates out, that was the cue to get going. She never failed to take me.

On top of everything else she's done for me, I could never thank her enough for that.

My entire family, plus spouses, came to the Sarajevo Olympics in February 1984. It was the first time the whole clan had been to a major competition and I was glad to have them there.

Sarajevo, where World War One started with an assassin's bullet, is in a valley in a mountainous area of Bosnia province. It's a fascinating mixture of old and new, where East meets West. Modern facilities mix with the Old City, which existed when Marco Polo passed through on his way to China. Several times every day you can see, and hear, the mullahs climb the minarets to summon the Moslems to prayer.

It had been an interesting six months leading up to Sarajevo.

I began to spend more time working in Toronto, at the Granite Club where Louis Stong, who was coaching Barb and Paul, ran his skating school. Just down the road was Glendon College, part of York University, where psychologist Peter Jensen had his office. Peter was working with a number of figure skaters, helping them prepare mentally for competitions, although I hadn't worked with him much.

Peter and Louis introduced me to Cybervision. In practice, whenever you do a perfect program, or individual elements, they're videotaped and kept for reference. The idea is that by studying yourself doing something flawlessly you get a mental picture of perfection that stays with you. It had a very positive, and confidence-building, effect on my psyche.

I spent time in Orillia that summer working with Karol Divin on figures, and I continued through the fall and winter to take lessons from Louis at the Granite Club. I was still doing the bulk of my skating in Orillia and Barrie with Doug, but I did spend a lot of time in Toronto. By 1985, those Toronto lessons had sort of dwindled away.

I had secured the music from *Cats*. I tried it on during a few exhibitions and decided to build my short program around it. Meanwhile, Uschi came up with the dramatic "King of Kings" music for the long. That was the beginning of what Doug, Uschi and I called "the total concept," in which the music, costume and program all melded into a single theme.

My Olympic short program costume was a brilliant yellow and black, with a design of an eye sewn into the shoulder. This tiger suit portrayed the cat-like theme magnificently. For the majestic "King of Kings" long program, the costume was an obviously regal purple.

"Total concept" had been building step-by-step, but in 1984 it all started to come together. As Uschi and I worked more together, and with the success of "Pink Panther," I was feeling very comfortable in interpreting music.

I won Skate Canada in October with a reasonable perform-ance. At Ennia Challenge Cup in Holland, I had two out-standing programs to win my second international. The ISU used Ennia that year for a judges' examination, so with all the big-time judges in attendance it was important to do well, which I did. This was the first time that I swept two fall events.

It was back home, then to Mannheim for two weeks of "cramming" with Uschi, then home for Christmas and to prepare for the Olympics and, almost as an afterthought, the nationals. For some reason I wasn't really training that well. I wasn't working as hard as I should have. I spent a lot of time in Toronto and went out some nights. I didn't go out a lot, but enough that it became a small distraction.

We flew into Regina in January and on the drive in from the airport a cold realization stung me: I wasn't ready for the nationals. I said to myself, "What am I doing here, I don't want to be here."

I was looking beyond Regina to the Olympics and therefore didn't skate at all well at the nationals. Gary Beacom won the figures and I was second, and the short program didn't significantly alter the standings. In the long, I did the axel but fell on the flip *and* the Lutz. I won narrowly and Gary was second, which put him on the Olympic team. Gordon Forbes was third, but they bypassed him for Sarajevo, choosing junior champion Jamiee Eggleton, instead. They gave Gordon a berth in the Worlds.

There was a lot of noise made to the effect that Gary should have won the championship. One national TV news show, W5 I think, did a segment on the nationals, hinting that the results might have been predetermined.

Although I would be the first to admit that I didn't skate up to my standard in Regina, I still think I won. But Gary missed some things and didn't have too much in the way of jumps, although the crowd liked his daring, off-beat program. He had had some disastrous programs in the past, so when he skated a reasonably good one, it shone by comparison.

Gary and I skated against each other for years, but we weren't friends. I never criticized his skating, but I felt that he criticized mine through the media.

Before the Olympics the whole Canadian team flew into Mannheim, where I felt right at home, for a training camp. It was my third time in Mannheim and there was plenty of ice time. The team was going into Sarajevo three or four days before the Opening Ceremonies, because the girls had to take the mandatory "femininity test," and the CFSA wanted to get the uniforms for the Opening Ceremonies, and make sure they all fit.

I just said, "Forget it," I wasn't going. We had confirmed flights into Sarajevo a couple of days later; there was plenty of ice time in Mannheim, and there wasn't much available in Sarajevo. For the first time, Doug really put his foot down with team officials, got angry, cursed, swore, and we didn't go. So, while we practiced in Mannheim, the team flew to Belgrade. But they ran into a snowstorm and had to take a bus through the mountains. They didn't get into Sarajevo until four or five in the morning. They were tired and cranky — but their uniforms fit. So did mine, as it turned out, and I took a two-hour flight into Sarajevo, having done all this extra skating.

The Opening Ceremonies were somewhat chaotic because they were a bit unorganized, but it was still a huge thrill. It was nothing like four years later in Canada, but still moving, especially as we marched past the Canadian contingent in the packed stadium.

I was confident heading into figures, and skated reasonably well, finishing seventh. For the first time, Scott won the figures; Jean-Christophe Simond was second; Rudi Cerne third; Jozef Sabovcik fourth; Aleksandr Fadeev (who won the European championship) fifth; and Heiko Fischer sixth. I was seventh and Brian Boitano and Norbert Schramm, paying the price, were in order behind me.

During the figures, Gary Beacom got mad at his marks, kicked the board and snapped at the referee. It became a huge international incident. It didn't affect me, although I was a little embarrassed for Canada about it.

Most of the Canadian media, except the two or three knowledgeable ones, had written me off as a medal contender, but I knew, and so did Doug, that there was a chance for silver. I just had to be second or better in the short and long (assuming Scott won both) and let the other pieces fall where they may.

During the pairs event earlier in the week, I noticed that many competitors went onto the ice looking scared to death. I didn't want that to happen to me, so when it was time for the short program, I decided not to skate cautiously.

I skated before Scott and Aleksandr, but after the other contenders, and it was the best short program I had ever delivered in my life. Everything was bang-on, especially the triple-Lutz combination. I was loose, and I think the judges finally made the connection between my music and the tiger-cat costume. I had exactly the same marks for technical as artistic — one 5.7, the others all 5.8s — which wasn't bad considering that two good skaters were yet to come.

Scotty didn't skate well. His camel spin wasn't good and he ran into the boards a couple of times on his footwork. He had skated well all week in practice, and we had been in awe that he had done everything perfectly. His program was safe and somewhat cautious, but good enough for second place.

That moved me up to fifth, although it was really a tie for third because Rudi Cerne, Jozef and I were separated by 0.4 points. Jean-Christophe had a good short (fourth) to stay second, and I needed to beat him by two positions to catch him. A gold was out of the question, unless I won the long and Scott finished fifth or worse, and no one had beaten him in a long program since *1980*. But a silver was a definite possibility.

I didn't think much about my chances. I was maintaining my composure well, just the right amount of nervousness to have an edge. I skated before Scott and Jozef in the long, and had a pretty good performance. It wasn't a perfect "total package," because I opened up a planned triple Salchow into a wide double. Other than that, it was very good, especially, I think, the slow portion where I piled up good marks. I was twenty-two then and full of energy. I just roared through my program, did a terrific triple axel, came off the ice to thunderous applause and got high marks. Scott popped a few jumps and didn't skate well (later we read that he had an ear infection), and Jozef skated well but tired near the end.

I had won the long program at the Olympics! With Scott second in the long and Jozef third, I had moved from seventh in figures to the silver medal. Scott won gold, Jozef bronze and the three of us went to the podium, just as we'd vowed eleven months earlier.

It was an emotional moment for me when I got that silver medal, and for my family, too. Evidently, they had been in the stands, crying with joy after the performance. It had been a great day for Canada. Earlier in the day, speedskater Gaetan Boucher had won his second gold medal of the Olympics. When I found out that I had won the silver, someone informed me that it was the best-ever finish by a Canadian male in Olympic figure-skating history. Somehow, that really burned home. I was excited not only by the medal, but also by how it was achieved. I had won *both* freeskating portions of the Olympic Games. Although my second-place finish would get under my skin four years later, it never occurred to me to be upset with that silver medal in Sarajevo. I was bursting with happiness and pride, and glad to have done it for Canada.

I was happy for Doug, happy for Uschi, and happy for my family. Actually my family had a close call before the Olympics. They went skiing in Austria. At the last moment, they had decided to forgo a trip to a ski hill that was later wiped out by an avalanche. I was glad that they had decided to come to Sarajevo, and that they could all be there to see the kind of pressure international athletes go through. Most of all, I was glad that I had shown them, and all Canadians, what I could do under pressure.

Coming off the Olympics, I was riding an incredible emotional high. I spent some time with my family after the competition, and came back to Orillia two weeks before Worlds, which were scheduled for Ottawa.

In one sense, it was beneficial to have Worlds in Ottawa, because I could come home and recover in familiar surroundings. Had they been elsewhere, it would have been a shorter and even more hectic time between competitions. But there was a drawback. After my Olympic success, expectations were heightened: some sports writers predicted that I would win the World championship on home ice.

Every fourth year, the top competitors find it very difficult to get psychologically motivated for Worlds, because they've just peaked for the Olympics. For that reason, the period between events is critical. To regain your intensity, you have to spend time alone, refocusing. I was worried because I didn't think I would be able to do that.

While figure skating is one of the most individual sports, it is also a group sport. Children begin in mass lessons of maybe thirty skaters. As the years pass, the groups are "pyramided" until, by the time the kids reach age twelve, there are only perhaps four or five of the original thirty still skating. Then local, regional and national competition begins in earnest. As a skater spends, by necessity, more time at the rink, he or she naturally turns away from schoolmates and toward other skaters for friendship. As the child becomes more involved with skating, so does the family. There are out-of-town competitions and practices. One or both parents might be involved in the local club executive. If a club plays host to a competition, they'll probably be volunteers and will meet other skaters and their families.

As the competition heightens both physically and emotionally, the number of skaters dwindles until, time after time, you begin to see the same faces. By 1984, it had been a dozen years since my first summer competition. I had been in dozens of events, soloed in scores of club carnivals, attended all kinds of seminars, partnered skaters through dance tests, and even done some judging. On each of those occasions, I came to know, and like, more skaters, parents, coaches, volunteers and members of media. It was entirely possible that, of the many Canadians who were fortunate enough to get tickets for Ottawa, I would know the vast majority. I began to worry that they would all expect to spend a few minutes with me.

Doug was probably more aware of this than I was and he made a difficult decision. I was to make myself scarce for the first time. I accepted no calls in my room. We held a daily press conference with smaller sessions to follow. No extra interviews, except for the *Orillia Packet and Times*. I would sign autographs before and after practice sessions, and hope that people would understand. Luckily, they did. Doug, and Teresa Moore of the CFSA – who many people feel is the best media-relations director in Canadian sport – formed my buffer zone, doing the tough talking for me and letting people down as easily as they could.

When I ran into Scott Hamilton, the night before the first practice, it was quite obvious that he didn't really want to be there. As a great American athlete, he had been under intense public scrutiny for years. Three world championships and an Olympic gold medal had taken their toll. He told other people that he had trouble getting up for the event, that it would be difficult for him in Ottawa because this was my country and I was the favorite skater. Everywhere else, Scott had been the favorite. There was a sense for him that he just couldn't win: if he lost, it would be an upset; if he won the gold, it was just the expected thing. I also think he wanted to prove that my two victories in freeskating at the Olympics had not been the natural course of things. Ottawa completed the bookends of his career. His first trip to Worlds was in Ottawa in 1978, when he finished eleventh, sandwiched between the two Canadians, Brian Pockar and Vern Taylor. His last trip to Worlds would also be in Ottawa. He told me that week that he was turning pro, and that it would be announced in a spectacular press conference in a few weeks, but I had the feeling that he would rather have turned pro right there.

Scott needn't have worried. By 10:00 A.M. of the first day of competition, he had his fourth gold medal in the bag, when he won figures and I finished seventh. My tracings were a little better than my average practice figures, and I usually skated a little below average in competition. I kept getting progressively better – I was seventh in left inside rocker, sixth in the right outside double-three, and fifth in the left back-change loop. Rudi Cerne was second. Heiko Fischer third, Jozef Sabovcik fourth, Aleksandr Fadeev fifth and Brian Boitano sixth.

While Scott didn't have to worry, I certainly did. Although I stood in the same position after figures as I did at Sarajevo, there were some significant differences. For one, Norbert Schramm wouldn't be in the freeskate to help out. With some true Schramm theatrics, he retired from amateur skating during the figures competition at Nepean Arena. After two figures he was eleventh. He took practice for the loop, but just before his turn he walked up to Sonia Bianchetti and quit. He told reporters that he didn't think he could finish any higher, and blasted the West German skating association for not supporting him. He said it was time to retire, but that his retirement was a protest against his association, too. Iron-ically, the first one to shake his hand was Gary Beacom, who'd delivered the outburst in Sarajevo during figures. It was Gary's turn to skate next. He finished eleventh, but I give him a lot of credit. He was calm, mentioned again that he skated only for himself, did a good combination in the short program to end up tenth over all. In fact with Gordon Forbes ninth, it was the first, and only, time that Canada had ever had three men in the Worlds' top ten.

Not only was Schramm out, there was one less weak freeskater above me, because Jean-Christophe Simond was not present. Boitano, whom I beat at Sarajevo, had moved ahead of me in figures. On top of that, we had forty-eight hours until freeskate — the organizers decided to place the off-day after figures, rather than after the short program.

Why, I don't know. There was really nothing to rest up from.

I drew to skate second last in the short program. I was fairly confident. This would be the fifth time I'd performed the short program in competition that year, and I'd won the other four.

The 1984 Worlds showed just how far the short program had come in two years. In 1982, I skated sixteenth from the end, and until the final two skaters, Schramm and Hamilton, I was the only one who didn't miss an element. After the warm-up in Ottawa, sitting in the dressing room under the stands, I could tell that all of the skaters ahead of me in the final group had done clean programs, and most of them were doing the triple-Lutz-double-loop combination. When somebody landed a combination cleanly, I could hear the crowd cheer loudly. The crowd reaction was more muffled for the other elements. I could sense the soft appreciation and clapping during the footwork sequences. Because I knew everyone else had done well, I was psyching myself up to do a perfect program, too.

After Scott skated, I came onto the ice to stretch. While he collected his flowers I couldn't help seeing his marks. They were all 5.8 and 5.9, except for one 5.7, and the crowd was standing.

Usually that doesn't bother me, but suddenly I got the jitters. My legs felt like jelly. I couldn't shake the nerves, even when the music started. I set up for the combination and began the glide for the Lutz, looking back over my shoulder. I must have tightened up, because I hung on to the glide too long. I pushed off the back foot into the Lutz, and I knew when I went up that I was in trouble. When I came out of the third rotation I was on an oblique angle, much too close to the boards, and it felt like I was coming down on the wrong foot. I knew I would have to do a three-turn — which would cost me 0.4 points — and could see myself out of the medals.

But when I landed, I was startled to find that I was on the

correct foot, although I thought I was still too close to the boards to get the loop in. But something inside of me said "jump" and I did. Somehow, I managed to dig in, pull the jump out and finish the program. I could hear the audience gasp. I think the anxiety of that near-fall took something out of them, because I really couldn't feel the crowd energy. They gave me a standing ovation, but I thought it was a reluctant one. I credit Doug's thoroughness with pulling me through that jump. In my mind, I had already resigned myself to a botched program, but hundreds and hundreds of combinations over the years had made it almost automatic for my body to go into the second jump.

I finished second to Scott in the short, although the Yugoslavian judge had me sixth, and that moved me into a tie for fifth with Heiko. Since only five men could skate in the final group the next night, they broke the tie by drawing numbers out of a bag. I drew number five and he drew six. It was a big break for me, to skate where the better marks were. I then drew to skate second in the final group, after Aleksandr, and directly before Scott.

The twenty-six hours before the freeskate were crammed with excitement and emotion. The pairs' freeskating final was held a few hours after our short program. Barb and Paul were sitting in second place behind the Russians, Elena Valova and Oleg Vassiliev. Barb had been my close friend for six years, and Paul had been my roommate during four World championships, including this one. They had gone through a severe depression after their disaster at the Olympics. They were on the verge of quitting one night at the Granite Club when they went out for one more skate, had a good runthrough, and decided to go to Ottawa.

Even though I had to freeskate the next night, I went to the Civic Centre. I wasn't going to miss the pairs' final. Valova and Vassiliev, the Olympic champions, skated well but left the door open. When Paul and Barb stepped out, everyone in the arena knew they had a chance to win the gold medal. After they landed a spectacular throw double axel — the move they fell on at Sarajevo — the crowd went crazy. For the final thirty seconds it was bedlam, and when they finished, everyone was yanked, screaming, to their feet because they knew Barb and Paul had won the gold medal. It was Canada's first gold medal since Karen Magnussen's in 1973, and the first on Canadian soil since Barb Wagner and Bob Paul's in 1960. They were both in the audience to see Barb and Paul win, as were Maria and Otto Jelinek, and Frances Dafoe and Norris Bowden, all the former World pairs champions from Canada. It was an incredibly emotional, intense night.

The next afternoon Jayne Torvill and Chris Dean gave the second-last performance of their amateur career, the final time they would do their famous "Paso Doble OSP" (Original Set Pattern, the equivalent of a singles short program). They were spectacular and got 5.9s for technical merit and 6.0s for artistic impression from all nine judges, putting them well over one hundred 6.0s for their careers.

By the time our final group skated, the audience was primed for a good show. The residue of excitement still lingered from Paul and Barb the night before, and Jayne and Chris had added to it. In the men's program, Gary Beacom and Gordon Forbes had both skated well, and had made it into the top ten. It was particularly gratifying for Gordon after having been left out of the Olympic team.

I had been feeling good all day, partly I guess because of the positive vibrations all around. I had a good warmup. Aleksandr skated first and was just finishing when I came out to take my skate guards off. He got good marks, but I concentrated on what I had to do. I skated to my start position and the music began. I was a little nervous going into the triple Lutz, but landed it cleanly. Then the adrenalin really started to pump: I wanted to get into the sit spin higher than I'd ever done before. I was a bit too pumped, and I leapt too high. I had to bail out. If that had been the day before, I would have been devastated, but I was much more confident today. And besides, the next element was the triple axel. I went into it, landed cleanly and I remember thinking as I came out of it that it had been the best I'd ever landed. The crowd must have sensed it, too, because they roared with the axel, then really got into the rest of the program. I could feel myself smiling as I went through the Salchow, flip, toe loop and other elements strongly. When I finished the crowd jumped to its feet. I felt a great weight lifted off my shoulders. Their reaction was spontaneous, not the reluctant, duty-bound, standing ovation of the day before.

My marks were all 5.8s and 5.9s, which, considering the missed sit spin and the fact that there were more guys to come, was nearly perfect.

Scott followed me this time, and had to look at *my* marks. He was a little sluggish and finished second in the freeskate, still easily the winner, and the first four-time Men's World champion since Hayes Alan Jenkins in 1956. I finished second, Fadeev was third, Sabovcik fourth, Cerne fifth and Boitano sixth.

When Scott was asked if he was retiring, he hedged a little, laughed, then said, "How many more years could I beat Brian Orser?"

It was the right thing to say in Canada, and I appreciated him saying it, but it made me realize that suddenly everyone was looking at me as his logical successor as World champion. I knew it wasn't that easy. Brian Boitano, Aleksandr Fadeev and Jozef Sabovcik were all in the hunt, too. I told the local paper that I thought three different men might win the title before the next Olympics. I assumed that I would be one of the three, and knew it would take a lot of work.

What I didn't know was how long it would take.

4. The Long Wait

To the casual observer, figure skating is anything but a year-round sport. You may never hear of it until late January when, suddenly, it's all over the television — Canadians, Europeans, U.S. nationals and Worlds — for about six weeks and then it disappears again.

To those inside skating, next year starts the morning after the World championships. My 1985 season — the year many Canadians assumed that I would finally win a World championship — began in Ottawa. Looking back, there were a few high moments rising above what was basically a terrible year.

Perhaps the best of the good moments came in Orillia in late June, three months after the World championships. Because of the ISU tour through North America, some carnivals I was committed to skate in, holidays and spring school at Twin Lakes Arena, Doug and I had been postponing some celebrations they wanted to have for us at home.

Orillia held a bit of a parade and an outdoor reception on the steps of the city Opera House between the Olympics and

Worlds, but wanted to do something bigger when the competition season was all over. I was representing solely the Mariposa Figure Skating Club by now, and that brought Orillia a great deal of national and worldwide recognition. But we were also training fairly regularly in Barrie; I grew up in Penetang and Midland; and my parents lived in Tiny Township. The County of Simcoe encompassed them all and every municipality and skating club in the area wanted to honor us for the silver medals.

I didn't know much about all this, but Doug did. He and Larry Simpson, Michelle's father, who was chairman of the Central Ontario Section of the CFSA knew that there was no way to fit everyone in. Spring and summer are the seasons when the important groundwork is laid for the next Worlds. So a cooperative effort was made to have all the municipalities get together at the Orillia Fair Grounds. The City of Orillia, Doug Little and Larry put it together.

It was kind of a who's who of skating with Rob McCall, Lloyd Eisler, Jamiee Eggleton, Paul Martini, Melinda Kuhnhegyi, Bernie Ford, Marilyn Symko, Karol Divin, Norris Bowden and Donald Jackson all there. My whole family was there and so were representatives of all levels of government. Johnny Esaw made a special trip to deliver a moving speech, and brought with him a video he had put together of my Olympic performance. Among the presentations was a scholarship established in my name by the Township of Tiny, and I guess the coup de grâce was administered by Orillia mayor Patricia MacIsaac. As she ended her speech she unveiled a huge picture of me in my "Cats" costume and said it would hang in the lobby of Twin Lakes Arena. Only it would no longer be called "Twin Lakes." As of that moment, it would be named "Brian Orser Arena."

I was flabbergasted. I can honestly say I had no idea that this was going to happen. Among the other presentations was a painting by a local Ojibwa Indian named Arthur Shilling. It was a wonderful portrait of a native woman and was appropriately titled "Spiritual Beginnings." Shilling, a major Canadian talent, who didn't receive as much recognition as he should have during his lifetime, died a couple of years later. Since his death, the painting has been appraised at over $18,000.

One of the other emotional presentations came from my longtime skate-maker John Knebli. He gave me a pair of boots and told the audience that he had sewn a piece of gold into the lining somewhere. The message was clear: when I won a gold medal, he would tell me where the gold was. If he should happen to die before I won, I would have to find it myself. I was determined to have him around to *tell* me where it was.

Later, Penetang renamed the lobby of the recently renovated arena — the same arena Mary Kay and I had a key to on those bitter mornings ten winters earlier — after me.

Those were big moments in my year, but if you consider what sort of year I was about to have, that is almost a backhanded compliment.

The season generally begins with the search for a program for the championships, which are still nine or ten months away. When it comes to a "game plan," as Doug likes to call it, figure skating differs from other sports. The planning is much more long term. Your main opponent is actually yourself. Can your four-and-a-half-minute long program and two-minute short be a smooth combination of the best moments you've had in hundreds of hours of practice? A competitive program is a series of tests, the difficulty of which you've decided yourself months before. A World-class skater's tests should be devised, and arranged, so as to push him to the limits of his skills, but not beyond. If he achieves this, and his skills are equal to or better than his opponents', *and* he can summon the best of himself at exactly the moment the music starts, then he will enjoy great success.

At a World championship, there are rarely last-minute changes to upgrade a program — it takes too many months of exact repetitions to perfect major tricks — although sometimes a skater will downgrade, or "skate safe," to avoid unneeded risks and secure his position. Therefore, the late spring and summer are critical times in the skating year. Your program has to be just right for you.

It is virtually taboo for a top skater to go back to Worlds with the same short and long program that he performed the year before. It's too much work to put two new programs together in the same year, and it's difficult to feel right at home with both, so we decided to keep "Cats" for the short program, and devise a new long program for the 1985 World championships in Tokyo.

I like to have a program for two years because it grows a lot. "Cats" had been outstanding in the Olympic year and I felt it could grow even more. A new costume design and the changed elements in the short program would alter it significantly, anyway.

I don't like to think about what the other skaters are doing. We examine closely where *I* want to be, and the kind of image I want to portray. For a couple of years, the idea had been to show another dimension of my skating, to show that I could express any kind of theme. "Fame," "Pink Panther," "Cats," "King of Kings" had differed widely from one another. One had shown grace, another dynamic power, another humor, another some classical elements. And in 1986, we would show traditional elements with the "Hungarian dance" short program. This varying of styles was something Brian Boitano also developed in time for the 1988 Olympics.

We finally decided upon a James Bond theme for the 1985 long program, because it was different than anything I'd done before. The music from *Octopussy* showed a different kind of power — understated. And in the middle of the program, we slowed things down and did a sexy blues theme, which was also new for me. The program was meant to portray caginess, sexiness, sudden power and coy humor, with James Bond as the vehicle.

Usually you start by assembling music. Back then, Uschi and I would talk about the concept and then it was in her hands. She would listen to music for hours on end at home, while she worked. Her husband, Aram, would bring dozens of records home from his store and she would tape anything she thought we could use. She would come to Orillia in June, usually with at least twelve and half minutes of music, and we'd start paring it down.

The next steps would be for me to listen to music and skate to it. I had developed artistically to the point that I could skate to the music and tell quickly if it was going to work. What sounds perfect in your living room can't always be transposed to an arena. We took out pieces that weren't suitable and carved our way down to four and half minutes.

Then we'd set to work on the actual outline of the program. Many times I'd hear a section of music, be grabbed by it and know what should go with it. I'd work on that section of the program then and there, setting the movements to it. There was no established order. It could be from any part of the program. In 1988, for example, the last thing I put together was the opening stance.

Although the programs change, basically many of the elements are in the same order. The triple Lutz and triple axel are dispensed with early, and dramatically, in the program in order to get them out of the way. They require a great deal of energy and the program can relax a little afterward.

By the end of June, the music is done and the skeletal order of the elements is in place. Some parts of the program mesh so well that they're set right away and they never change. Other parts are designed and you say to yourself, "Well, they're not perfect, but they'll grow." And, as you do your program more and more, they do evolve, nuances are added, you change a few things and you get a real feel for the program.

You don't always carry your program around in your head — although I did in 1988 — but it's with you a lot. You play it at least once, maybe three or four times, a day. I was always fine-tuning it in the first half of the season. By August I would be ready to show it to a couple of Canadian judges and Barbara Graham when they came up to Orillia. They would make suggestions and offer some positive criticism. It is always a little tough to let go of the previous program, especially if you've done well with it. In 1984, David Dore suggested to me that I hang on to the "Fame" short program, because it was going to be hard to top. But I'd done it for two years, and had decided upon "Cats," which did top "Fame." To grow you have to change. To be fully committed to the program, I really have to make up my own mind when it comes to what I'll skate to.

In the fall, it's time to take the program on the road. One of the main functions of the fall competitions is to try the program out on international judges and try to sense their reaction. It's a very nerve-wracking time because it sets the tone of acceptance you'll likely receive at Worlds, although sometimes an individual judge can be way off base. For instance, before the 1986 season, a Canadian judge told me at one competition that my program was terrible, that Uschi didn't design good programs. But we were determined to keep it, and we did, for two years. The next year, the same judge said the program was a much better vehicle for me. Of course, it was exactly the same program.

In the fall competitions, especially St. Ivel which is so early, it's hard to come up with your best routine. Your program is still in its raw form. It hasn't grown at all. You haven't added your own flavor to it and it's very mechanical but *you* know it will blossom in the following months of diligent practice.

Since the St. Ivel that saw my program a minute too short, I've never made a major change during or after the fall season. As each year went on I would get a better feel for the program earlier in the year. I knew what I was doing, knew there was a reason for each movement and was maturing both as a skater and as a person.

Psychological preparations for the fall skates are similar to the Worlds, although with far less pressure to cope with. You have to hit a certain arousal level for each program. There are very narrow boundaries for the short, which is very quick and energetic and almost hyper. You have to be calmer for the extended, more demanding long program, but you still must be in a certain zone of arousal. The boundaries are wider, however, than those for the short.

There is some psyching-out among competitors before an event, but not much at the higher levels. In my time the only real attempt at that usually came from Heiko Fischer, who has been trying it for years. He even tried it the night before the 1988 Olympics opened, when he needled me about figures.

The fall of the 1984-85 season, I competed at Skate Canada, which I won with a below-average performance against a mediocre field. I had somehow lost my triple axel. This was the only time it happened to me in my career, and the spell lasted all through September and October. I suffered major stress over that stupid triple axel. I had lost the timing and just couldn't do one. Eventually, it came back.

Then I went to NHK in Tokyo, at the same rink where the Worlds would be held a few months later. The major competition came from Aleksandr Fadeev, who was skating very well. Unlike other Canadians, I wasn't taking anything for granted. I had never assumed that I would just be handed the 1985 World title. I knew that there were other great skaters out there.

Fadeev was awesome at NHK, just as good as he would be at the Worlds in March. I didn't skate well and he won. He did a triple axel combined with a double toe loop in his long program and was working on a triple-Lutz-triple-toe-loop combination. Strong stuff. I never seem to skate well in Japan. For two years, whoever beat me at NHK in November would win the Worlds in March.

Looking back, I made a mistake that year in taking too many exhibition dates and not working hard enough at training my figures. I was honoring requests from all over the world, skating in western Canada, Denmark, Germany and France around Christmas, and I ran myself down.

I skated well at Canadians in Moncton, earning one 6.0 in the short and seven in the long; four for technical, three for artistic; but I may have left my best performance there.

Enormously fatigued from all the travel, I was susceptible to sickness. Just before the Worlds, I caught pneumonia. I was still suffering from it when the competition started, but I didn't say anything to the papers because I didn't want to be a complainer. Over all, it was a terrible week in Tokyo. I was sick. The rink was too far from the hotel and could only be reached through clogged traffic. The rink itself was cold and wretched. It was actually the swimming pool from the 1964 Olympics and it made a terrible THUNK sound when you came down on the ice, which was too hard. And aesthetically, it was a mess — a terrible streaked-blue color. It was also quite a distance from the stands, which destroyed any chance to establish a rapport with the crowd, a disappointingly small one. Everyone else had to put up with the rink conditions too, of course, and it sure didn't bother Fadeev. It just wasn't my week.

I was fourth in figures, which Aleksandr won. When he also won the short program, the event was over for me. At least two other skaters, besides me, would have had to beat him for me to win the gold. As it was, it was going to be hard for me to win even the silver.

I was scheduled to skate last in the long program. With my

hands on my face, through parted fingers, I watched Fadeev skate. He started off like a dynamo, with a triple Lutz-triple loop and triple axel-double toe loop, and I knew I couldn't win.

It was difficult to psyche myself up to skate after that, but I had had to skate my best to finish second before, so I tried. This time was a little different, because this was the year I was supposed to win. I didn't skate badly, but it wasn't magical. I squeaked out the axel, did the flip and Lutz and didn't go down on anything, but it wasn't nearly as good as Fadeev. He was superb, and he deserved to be World champion.

During the week, the CFSA promoted me through daily press releases. These were designed partly to give the media background information so that I wouldn't be hounded by the same questions over and over again. This was a real concern. Aleksandr didn't need those releases to fend off the media because the Russians simply didn't talk to the media during the event. After I lost, Michael Cosgrove wrote a scathing article in the *Globe and Mail* about the releases and how they came at the cost of the other members of the team. He suggested that I would always be a second-place finisher. Michael seems to be a very bitter man and it might have given him some solace to write that article, but the rest of the team was incensed by it and so were a lot of Canadian skating fans.

I had learned a lesson in Tokyo: nothing comes easily. On coming home, I decided that we would have to have *two* new programs for 1986.

It bothered me that someone else was World champion. In the new program, I would have *two* triple axels, and one of them would be in combination with a *triple* toe loop. A triple axel had never been done with a triple jump and no one had ever done two triple axels in the same program, but I had a statement to make. I wanted to show that, despite the growth in my artistry, I was still on the leading edge of technical skating.

I worked my butt off after that, taking a lot of positive steps: harder and longer practices, stricter discipline, even more dedication than before.

In the fall, I won St. Ivel again, showing the new programs — the "Hungarian dance" short program, and the theme from the movie *Ladyhawke* in the long. Then we returned to Japan for the NHK competition. Again, I had back luck in the East. I fell on the axel and lost to Brian Boitano because of that fall.

But Canadians went well in North Bay, Ontario, and for the first time I finished first in all three figures. The year before, my sixth year at nationals, was the first time I had won the figures competition.

The World championships were to be held in Geneva in March, and I headed overseas full of confidence, and ready to try to take the title away from Aleksandr Fadeev.

The 1986 World championship in Geneva began with a small housing crisis. An OPEC conference whose participants had booked much of the Hotel Internationale had necessitated a shuffling of accommodation for North American tours and media, although this had little effect upon the skaters. The double-tiered lobby of the elegant hotel was, however, filled with robed Arabs being hotly pursued by network cameras.

Doug Leigh became friendly with an OPEC bodyguard who took a sudden interest in figure skating and even arranged for tickets for the freeskate. However, Leigh made the mistake of asking the man about his occupation. "For your living you teach skating," the man grinned. "For my living I kill people."

Another member of the Canadian team had an equally harrowing experience in the hotel. A thief broke in while she and her roommate slept and made off with her jewellery.

The shaky start to the week may have been an omen of what was to befall Brian Orser himself, but there was a positive atmosphere in Geneva throughout training. He was skating well, he felt good and, for the first time, he could sense a feeling among judges he encountered that this was to be Brian Orser's year.

Prospects were not as rosy for Johnny Esaw, executive vice-president of CTV sports.

Since 1962 he had been the acknowledged godfather of Canadian figure skating. Every one of the young men and women representing Canada in Geneva that week had grown up listening to Esaw describe figure-skating events, hoping that one day they would be the ones he interviewed.

CTV went on the air January 1, 1961, and sports was a big part of its focus. In summer their schedule was filled with Canadian professional football; winters featured international hockey and a program that would become a broadcasting legend — ABC's Wide World of Sports. And there was figure skating. It was a "special event" in CTV parlance, but "it was the biggest, by far, special event we had." In 1960 Esaw negotiated the television rights to the World championship, held in Vancouver, at the request of ABC. The American network felt that a Canadian broadcaster — even though Esaw was as yet without a network — would not have to pay such exorbitant rates. And they were right. Esaw got the rights for a paltry $10,000 and turned them over to ABC. In the latter half of the 1980s, American rights would command between $1.5 and $2 million. The two networks eventually worked together and the first World skating championship CTV carried was ABC's production of the 1962 event from Prague, Canada's most successful ever. Since then, CTV had broadcast the World championship, with Esaw as the lead commentator, every year except 1966. And that included 1985, just six months after Esaw's quadruple-bypass heart operation.

Over the years, Esaw and the Canadian Figure Skating Association became indelibly intertwined. When Esaw left the broadcast booth to concentrate on front-office duties as executive vice-president in charge of sports, figure-skating season was the only time he climbed behind the mike. Much of the CFSA's expanding financial base — from which the ability to develop skaters comes

— could be attributed to a two-way CTV deal with the CFSA that offered sponsors a package of television, program and board ads for Skate Canada and the national championships. To keep the money in Canada, CTV paid well for these events, and bid low for the World-championship rights. But the International Skating Union, not the CFSA, awards world rights. When the Canadian Broadcasting Corporation put in an impressive final bid earlier that year, of $1.6 million for four years, far higher than the annual $100,000 CTV had been paying, Esaw refused to enter a matching bid, calling the process blackmail. Shaken, he bitterly accused CBC of going after figure skating in retaliation for CTV's getting involved in NHL hockey that year. The CBC countered that the CTV had been paying well below market value for skating. The end results were that the CBC landed a four-year contract to televise the Worlds, beginning in 1987; the CFSA entered a protest, not against the CBC, but against the practice of a national association not being allowed to take part in negotiations for World-championship rights in its own country: and the occasional CBC executive strode through the corridors in Geneva sizing up the territory.

The weekend of March 20-22 would be Johnny Esaw's last broadcasting a World championship. He wanted to go out the same way he had come in — with a winner. Brian Orser winning a World championship would put the other bookend on CTV's World coverage. Their first year saw Donald Jackson win; their last, he hoped, would see Orser win.

In Orser, Esaw recognized the same commitment to success that he had seen in Jackson, the same artistry, the same pioneering technical ability. He had been a friend of the Orsers for ten years, had helped cultivate Brian's on-camera presence, had been the keynote speaker at his Olympic-medal dinner in Orillia.

There is a certain ambience to every figure-skating competition that makes it unlike any other before or after. It is an extremely personal feeling. No two skaters would make exactly the same observations about the intense two weeks that make up practice and the actual competition. In Tokyo, for instance, I had the haunting sense of being looked upon with disfavor. In Geneva, it was exactly the opposite. I had the distinct impression that everyone, especially the judges, wanted me to win, regardless of what had happened the previous year or at NHK.

Despite that, the first day of competition didn't bode well for any shot at the gold medal. You have to make a positive impression on the first figure and I didn't. Two judges had me as high as fourth on the figure, but the Soviet judge (Tatiana Danilenko) put me fourteenth and I was eighth over all on that first figure. Over my career I never complained about judging, at least not publicly, but I always felt that a great figures reputation helped you. Heiko, Jozef and Fadeev all made a few mistakes that year, but weren't penalized for them. With me and some of the others, they looked for things to knock down; with some they looked for things to build up.

My traditionally poor figure, the double-three, was coming up and I had five hours to think about it. I went back to the hotel, had breakfast, watched a French movie and tried to time it to come back just in time to put on my skates and do the figure. I did a good second and third figure to move up to fifth, one spot down from the year before and behind, in order, Fadeev, Sabovcik, Heiko Fischer and Brian Boitano. A lot of people wrote me off again as a gold-medal hope.

For me to be champion I had to win both the short and long programs and somebody else would also have to beat Aleksandr and Jozef in one event each. I still thought it was in reach. What outsiders didn't know, that I did, was that Aleksandr and Jozef weren't skating well. I had good practices and there were some other good freeskaters like Boitano and Vladimir Kotin who could help out.

The short program went according to plan. I skated to a Hungarian number and finished first, winning five judges, while Fadeev was second with four. Kotin was great and took care of Jozef for me by finishing third, while Jozef was fourth.

So, heading into the long program, I was third overall with 3.4 placement points, following Fadeev (1.4) and Sabovcik (2.8).

I needed to win the long and have somebody else finish ahead of Aleksandr, which I thought could easily happen. Brian Boitano was fifth in the short and fourth over all, but could still turn in a technically sound long, and Kotin was having a very good week. And Jozef might come up big, although I doubted it.

For some reason — perhaps because I'd never actually been in contention for a gold medal on the final day — on the day of the long program, I changed my routine. I don't normally try to kill time, but on this day I did, and toured Geneva on foot with my family. Since my first World championship, I had taken a solitary walk on the day of the long program, although I didn't realize how important that ritual was. I had started the habit because my body had told me to take a walk, and each year thereafter I did it. But when I got back to the hotel, I decided not to take the walk, because I'd been walking so much of the day, and didn't want to get tired. I would forgo the mental benefits in order to preserve my leg strength.

There were other little things. Normally, I don't cut my nails during a competition. It's sort of a Samson-haircut kind of superstition. That afternoon, I bit them. Tore them all right off. It was a little bit of nerves, and also, perhaps, some kind of rebellion.

To backtrack a little, I should mention that I was a little psyched out by the triple axel. Before Geneva, the team had spent five days training in Mégève and, in order to pay for half of our ice time, it was agreed that we would skate an exhibition for the French villagers. I was totally against it — the timing could not have been worse — but I had no choice.

I fell on the triple axel for the first time in months. Not since NHK had I had any problems with it. After that, I was still landing them and landing the triple-axel-triple-toe-loop combination in my runthroughs, but I admit I was psyched out.

On that final day, I also wasn't as nervous as I should have been, wasn't pumped up, wasn't into it. For the first time in my career, I was in contention for the gold medal and I was wondering how to handle it. I thought that I should be cool. I didn't *want* to be nervous.

All these things — not taking a walk, biting my nails, psyched out by the axel, not being nervous — sound minute, but figure skating is a precise sport and you must stand and deliver at the appointed time. A full year comes down to that four and a half minutes. You not only have to *be* right, you have to *feel* right. Nervous habit and rituals all contribute to lessening the burden you carry.

When I got to the rink, all of a sudden BANG, I was nervous. It hit me all at once and I didn't have time to deal with it and let it take its course.

I was skating fourth in my group, after Fadeev, Boitano and Jozef. Surprisingly, I had a good warm-up, but then had to wait for my turn. Doug, Uschi and I went into a make-up room under the stands and I could hear the sounds from the arena, making me even more nervous. I snapped at them to turn on the shower full blast to drown out the noise so I wouldn't know what was happening. I thought I was doing the right thing at the time.

What Brian Orser could not possibly have known as the shower spray drummed reality out of the dressing room was that a drama of immense passion was being played out on the ice.

Aleksandr Fadeev took the ice first among the contenders and he crumpled under the pressure of retaining his crown against what many observers called the best skating field in history. He skated miserably: two-footed his triple axel, fell outright on his triple loop, fell again and made only three triples cleanly.

The crowd was stunned, but they were mortified moments later when Soviet judge Tatiana Danilenko — the same judge who had Orser fourteenth in the first figure and who would later be suspended by the ISU and her own federation — awarded him a preposterous 5.9 for technical merit.

The crowd hooted, whistled and stamped its collective feet in derision. Then, almost as one, they noticed Brian Boitano removing his skate guards. The irony was too delicious. After the most blatant case of favoritism — by a Soviet judge — in recent memory, the next skater was an American.

The crowd turned its affection to Boitano more strongly than could have been expected. And he responded. Although his choreographic execution was still a little wooden, he was technically superb, landing a triple-axel-double-toe-loop combination early and blazing his way through five other triples. It was a spectacular performance and he moved into first place.

Fadeev was now fourth, and falling, in the long, and out of the running. It was the break the Canadian needed. Sabovcik withered in his performance and when Brian Orser stepped onto the ice, it was the first time in his life that he had come to his final program of a season with an opportunity to win the gold medal.

Only he didn't really know it.

When it was my turn to skate and I came down the tunnel to the ice surface, I had a sense that there was a chance to win if I skated well. You could tell from the way people acted as I walked by them. That made me even more nervous . . . . Again, I didn't know how to handle it.

Just before they announced my name, another of those silly little things, which I let get to me, occurred. A gold chain I wear around my wrist came loose. Something inside of me said that I *had* to wear it. I tried to do it up, couldn't, and then skated over to Uschi and barked at her to do it up. She was shaking and neither of us could manage it. I think I lost my focus right then and there.

I was still trying to deal with this when the public-address system suddenly announced, "Next skater, Brian Orser, Canada." I didn't have my usual pre-skate moment in which I pump myself, clench my fists and focus my thoughts on my performance.

But the first jump, the triple Lutz, was clean and solid. I moved toward the other end of the rink, circled in to do the triple-axel-triple-toe combination and everything felt in sync. I turned forward onto my left foot, planted and took off for the six-and-a-half-revolution jump that had never been done in any competition.

As Brian bent his left leg, to begin the familiar maneuver that was his calling card, Johnny Esaw leaned into the jump with him, hoping to influence the final outcome with a little body English. In the CTV *television booth, which was located in the stands opposite the spot on the ice where a hockey blue line would be, Esaw — the equivalent of hockey's play-by-play man — was flanked by color commentators Brian Pockar and Debbie Wilkes who knew, better than Esaw perhaps, what the Canadian skater was going through.*

But this had been a particularly emotional week for Esaw. He had butterflies in his stomach. He was convinced that he was less than five minutes from seeing something he had been waiting twenty-three years to see again — a Canadian men's World champion. As the pounding beat of Orser's music mounted toward the crescendo that signalled the triple-axel-triple-toe-loop combination, which would be attempted just below his broadcast booth, Esaw didn't speak much. He let the picture tell the story. Orser entered the jump and Wilkes and Pockar suddenly moaned, "Oh no!"

The Canadian champion had inexplicably crashed to the ice on the triple-axel portion of the combination and was scrambling

madly to his feet, visibly shaken, trying to regain his momentum
and place in the program.

"It was like a poke in the stomach," Esaw would say later. "The
odds had been very, very high against the door opening for Brian,
and there it was suddenly opened and then .... Oh God, the
hollowest, most sickening feeling you've ever had."

It just took me by surprise. To this day I have no idea what
happened. Something just went wrong.

I may have been a little over-anxious. This would be the
first triple axel ever combined with a triple jump, but I had
been landing them all week in practice, so there was no
reason why I shouldn't have made it. Looking back on it, my
free leg was a little high, but I'm sure that I'd done that in
practice, too, and landed the combination. I also didn't like
the full floppy sleeves on my costume — I have always
preferred the streamlined look — and I remember looking at
them as I skated and trying to adjust my arm position so that
they wouldn't flop so much, even as I went into the jump. But
none of that should have mattered. I just tumbled and there
was no way to figure it out.

I was right down on the ice. I had to find my feet and catch
up to the program again. I probably missed about five seconds and during that whole time I could hear the audience, as
one, moaning a shocked, "Oooohhhh." That's the worst
sound I ever heard.

From that point on it was a catchup game, being cautious. I
doubled a triple flip, but still had a chance to salvage something, because I had the second triple axel planned. But I
fumbled out of that, too. I didn't have a whole lot of confidence left, although I said to myself, "I've got to nail this, I've
got to nail this." But when things don't go well from the start,
you don't have the feeling or flow, and it becomes very
mechanical and cautious.

I finished and knew I had lost. I was disappointed more in

not skating well than in not winning. I didn't deserve to win. As I skated off, one of the officials told me I was second, and I assumed that Fadeev had won again. That's how much I knew about what had gone on before me.

I looked at the official and said, "Fadeev?" and he said, "No, Boitano." I put my face in my hands. I was shocked. I always knew Brian was an outstanding competitor, but I hadn't yet thought of him as World champion. I considered myself better than him. But he deserved to win that day — he skated great. He was the only one who delivered a clean program, and they had to give it to him. He earned it fully.

After it was over, I was extremely disappointed in myself. I wasn't sure that I would ever have such a great opportunity again. It had been offered to me on a silver platter — right there. I could see that the judges wanted me to do it and I didn't produce. I was distressed that I didn't skate well. That's the worst feeling in skating, when you don't produce. I didn't feel that way after the 1988 Olympics, but it was a terrible, burning taste in 1986.

We went over for dope testing in an adjacent arena. I recall pointing toward the darkened rink and saying, over and over again, "I could go out there now do ten of those axels." It was such a feeling of frustration. And that helplessness would be rekindled each night on the ensuing ISU tour when it was Brian Boitano, not Brian Orser, who got to do his exhibition skate last among the men. I had won the ISU gold medal in the freeskate, but it was a hollow victory. Give Brian credit: he did it when it counted. He was the best that night.

If there was any consolation, it came in the reception audiences gave me at the exhibition in Geneva and on tour. I started working on a back-flip, which is illegal in competition skating, just before Christmas in the parking lot outside the arena in Orillia. I worked on the technique with a local school teacher and after a couple of sessions with the training belt, I had it. It's a move that Robin Cousins uses on pro tours, but it's not simple. Norbert Schramm mistimed one and smashed his face in. But the crowd loves it, and when I unveiled it at Geneva, it was gratifying to hear the applause.

It was on tour that I decided to seek out the help of Peter Jensen, the sports psychologist who was working with other skaters on the Canadian team. I realized that I was having trouble dealing with the possibility of winning.

British writer John Hennessy wrote of the missed axels, "Canadians felt it went against some law of nature." I had made my name with the triple axel. It seemed ironic that it should cost me a World title.

Having been thrown when I was close to the finishing line, I just had to get back on the horse again. But the next competition was seven months away, and the next Worlds an agonizing year in the future.

5. Top of the Podium

Three times Brian Orser had been runner-up at the world championship. He had also finished second at the Olympics and while these were all significant achievements, there could be no escaping that now that the Canadian public was finally taking note of the small-town Ontario boy, they were also wondering, some aloud, about his ability to win it all.

The history of men's singles has been sprinkled with multiple second-place finishes. At the turn of the century, the great Ulrich Salchow was runner-up twice before going on to win ten world titles in succession. Willy Bröckl of Austria was second three times and third once before starting a four-year winning streak in 1925. Karl Schäfer was second twice, then won it seven straight times. Britain's Graham Sharp was second three times before winning his only title in 1939. Donald Jackson twice settled for silver before finally winning Canada's first gold medal in 1962. Alain Calmat of France was second twice before he, too, won in 1965.

But for Brian Orser, skating history also had a darker side. There had been others, generally skating in the shadow of long-time champions, who could never take that last stride up the podium steps. Heinrich Burger, Max Bohatsch, Otto Preissecker, Roger Turner and Ernst Baier were each twice runners-up in the sport's earlier years and retired without a title. Tim Brown of the United States had two silvers but never won, and Jimmy Grogan, skating behind legends Dick Button and Hayes Jenkins, finished second four consecutive years without taking the Big One.

"It was important not to get down," Jackson recalled. "I finished third in the 1960 Olympics at Squaw Valley, and when the top two didn't go to Worlds at Vancouver, I was expected to move up and win." But Jackson finished second to Alain Giletti in the 1960 Worlds. When the 1961 event was cancelled because of the plane crash near Brussels which killed the entire u.s. team, he had to wait until 1962 to take the final step to skating immortality.

To be able to continue financially, Jackson moved his training from New York to Toronto and began working with Sheldon Galbraith. A by-product of that move was that he was working with several top-ranked skaters, including World pairs champions Otto and Maria Jelinek and Bob Paul and Barbara Wagner. "I felt inspired, and that gave me confidence and the change of atmosphere was good, too," said Jackson.

Brian Orser would make several changes in his training regimen for 1987, too, but one burning question still lingered from 1986. Should Doug Leigh and Uschi Keszler have told him that he needed only to skate a safe program to win the World title in Geneva? Before he skated out for his dramatic win in 1962, Jackson had asked Galbraith if there was a chance to pull into first. His coach had said, "There's room at the top."

Orser had consistently told his coach that he didn't want to know how other skaters had done. That wish was underlined by the incident with the shower spray. Doug Leigh said it was impossible not to know that he had a chance to win: "When we came out, everyone was pressed against the walls, almost two-dimensional, with their mouths open, looking at us." But should Leigh have taken a chance and told his skater to scrub a triple-triple combination that had never been landed?

Doug did absolutely the right thing in not telling me what the situation was. If he had told me, I probably would have said we'd go right ahead with it. The triple axel-triple toe loop had been consistent in practice all week, and that's what we were basing decisions on. Hindsight is 20-20, and you could argue that I should have been told just to skate safely, but if I had landed the combination the performance might have been judged one of the greatest of all time, like Donald Jackson's. People would then have looked at Doug as a brilliant tactician for not advising me to be conservative. I'm not good with last-minute changes, and Doug, more than anyone, is aware of that. If he had told me to skate cautiously, and *that* had caused me to skate poorly, it would have been even worse.

After my experience in Geneva, I knew that my problem was a mental one. I had never been so physically ready in all my life, but something psyched me out, something took my focus away from skating. Immediately upon my return to Canada, I called Dr. Peter Jensen.

We'd had sports psychologists around figure skating for years, but I thought they were kind of hokey and unnecessary. I had even participated in some of Peter's relaxation and imagery-group gatherings, but I wasn't too impressed. I had been against it in principle, and went into the sessions with a closed mind. I felt that the sessions made me too nervous about competition too early in the season. Plus, at the time, I really didn't think it was essential.

Now I knew I needed some help, and started working with Peter right away.

Peter and I dissected every one of my competitive performances, separating them into good and bad, and searching for common threads. That was when we determined that a pre-competition walk on my own was a key factor. I hadn't done that in Geneva.

Bad performances were characterized by not sticking to my normal patterns: not going for the walk in Geneva; getting to the rink too early; not putting on my costume in the hotel room to walk through my program — things like that. The bad performances often involved Canadian championships, all, for some reason, in western Canada — Brandon, Victoria, Regina — and Worlds in Geneva. Some of the Canadian performances can be explained away by the overshadowing presence of the big World event to follow. In fact, some of my best efforts at nationals were followed by less spectacular deliveries at Worlds.

Peter also put me through a lot of group relaxation techniques involving imagery. The lights would be off and soft music playing, and he'd talk us through a color session. We'd be on an elevator going floor to floor: a red number one, blue number two, and so on, and then we'd climb on a magic carpet and fly off to a peaceful place.

A lot of times we would just fall asleep and wouldn't remember hearing anything. We had sessions at Glendon College in the off-season and they were offered every night during a competition.

We were always practicing this kind of mental imagery, so if I wanted to apply it to my skating, I had already gone through the process. I could more easily picture a jump in my mind, or even my whole program. I could bring myself to the proper "arousal level" quite readily. Arousal level basically describes how hyper you want to be for a performance.

We also worked on simulations of a competition day. In Orillia, Barrie, Kitchener or wherever, we'd have an announcer, people watching, six-minute warm-ups, everything as close as possible to the trappings of a normal championship. Doug and I had done simulations before, especially for figures, but with Peter we *really* got into it. Before Worlds, we even rented Maple Leaf Gardens and brought in Wilf Langevin, who announces national, international and World championships. We'd have people there with noise-makers or cameras, all trying to distract me. We simulated everything — different skating positions, the skater before me taking too long picking up his flowers. We even had a television crew from CBS obnoxiously block my way in my walkthrough while they were up for a (real) filming session.

From these simulations, we found that if I was skater number three, I'd do best with a walkthrough of the program while number one was on. If I skated first, I did it before warm-up, and so on, all the way down the line. We also found that for my short program, I'd like to have an arousal level of "9" while for the long I wanted a "7.5" or so, because it's not such a sprint. Peter would establish eye contact with me and ask where I was. If I was too low, he'd help pump me up; too high he'd bring me down, somehow. I don't even know what it was that he said.

I told Peter about the missed axel in Mégève and how I had convinced myself that it was an omen. The problem was that I hadn't let anyone in on it; there was no external release, and so the tension built up. From that point on, I was to tell him about all my doubts, no matter how trivial they seemed. Almost every World-class athlete experiences fear of failure. That's the worst part of the idle day before the long program — you're always picturing the worst. And then you become afraid.

Even after working with Peter, I experienced that fear, but I recognized it and dealt with it. It's part of competition. Not dealing with reality is absolutely the wrong way to handle it. We worked on taking it as it comes, good, bad or otherwise. You walk in and hear the crowd and know what's happening. Period. You don't have to wonder what's going on and you don't deliberately flee from it.

There was a lot of criticism that I depended too much upon Peter Jensen. In fact, I spent only one and a half seasons with him and it was me, not him, doing the actual skating. Most of our work together was done long before the competitions. Peter didn't have to be there, but I like him to be. He was a neutralizing force upon Doug and Uschi and me. He was someone to unload on. People are afraid of sports psychologists — I was — and I think that's the source of much of the criticism.

So I spent much of that season reworking my emotional and mental state for competition. At the same time, I was also making some physical changes.

One of the major physical changes came about through another important member of our family: my dad's older (by one year) sister, Kathy. As she and my dad were growing up, they were very close. My grandfather was off in the navy, and my grandmother would be with him so, in a way Kathy and my dad raised each other. When she was sixteen, Aunt Kathy contracted rheumatoid arthritis and was eventually confined to a wheelchair. Undaunted, this strong-willed woman later moved to California and obtained her doctorate in law.

She was quite an inspiration to all of us. We knew how sick she was, and could only imagine what kind of pain she endured, but we never heard her complain. She moved to Midland, and she helped my parents make a lot of their business decisions. We all became close to her.

In California, one of Aunt Kathy's best friends had been a physiotherapist named Helen James. They somehow lost touch with each other for ten years. In the mid-eighties, they renewed their friendship and Helen — whose last name prompted the moniker "Jimmer" — began travelling up to Midland to administer the physiotherapy that her old friend required.

I met Jimmer through Kathy, and she talked to me about a form of therapeutic deep massage called rolfing. It sounded like a side-effect of the flu, but I was intrigued. Jimmer, who was then sixty-seven years old, had been a rolfer for six years. She explained to me that while physiotherapy dealt more with joints and muscles, rolfing concentrates on the soft tissues that hold the muscles and bones in place.

Jimmer explained that the main goal of rolfing is to reduce stress by aligning the body properly with gravity. It was, she said, easy to get out of alignment with gravity through bumps and bruises to the tissues, or through poor posture. The tissue tightens and the body gets out of alignment and you have to waste muscle power to keep from falling with gravitational force. In rolfing, the tightening is released in an orderly, sequential fashion. That reduces stress, and gives the body more flexibility and mobility.

Given what happened in Geneva, and the general tightness I sometimes felt in competition, I decided to give it a try.

It's difficult to describe — it's a very deep massage. Once in a while it hurt, but after a few sessions, I could feel the rolfing work on me and my body somehow felt right. I started feeling lighter on my skates. And, believe it or not, I actually "grew," from five-six-and-a-half to five-seven.

Much was made in the press about my rolfing sessions but they were important to my physical and psychological well-being. Jimmer and I could really communicate. By watching me closely, she could tell right away when I had a bump or bruise, and where I felt tight. She knew when I was out of alignment and probably knew my body better than I did. Jimmer and I became good friends and that brought me even closer to my aunt. It was touching for her to see me so connected to her dear friend.

The ravages of her illness finally overcame her and Aunt Kathy died the next year, in September 1987. It was the first time anyone close to me had died and I was devastated; we all were. My dad had a very difficult time getting over it. But Jimmer stayed on our "team" and was a living reminder of

Aunt Kathy. It was as if she was with us in spirit.

In addition to the rolfing, I started to change my food regimen. I had never been a junk-food addict and had always eaten well, but an American nutritionist, Ann Hall, approached me about a new diet. She visited me and sent me food. After about a year I didn't see her again, but I stuck to the diet. In fact, I went at it even more rigorously.

Sometimes the diet became an inconvenience. What I needed to know about the chemistry of food and the body took hours to learn, and I didn't have hours.

The diet allows no fried foods and very little red meat, neither of which was much of a sacrifice for me. It includes lots of fish and chicken.

I ate a lot of raw vegetables, as many as possible organically grown. Every morning I would have oats and granola in freshly squeezed orange juice, with organic raisins and a sliced banana thrown in. At lunch I'd make one of my "power shakes" in the blender: protein powder, brewer's yeast, an egg, a banana, freshly squeezed orange juice, carob, lecithin and honey. It was a real power-booster. I could feel it. For snacks, Ann also made me some "power balls" made of almond butter, organic peanut butter, a bit of honey, brewer's yeast, protein powder, coconut and nuts. Now I make them myself.

When I detailed my daily diet, Frank Orr of the *Toronto Star* quipped, "It's enough to choke a buzzard," but I like it. It definitely made me feel better and my weight remained right at 133-34 pounds.

My new concern with nutrition walked hand in hand with some non-skating concerns, too. I had wanted to get involved in something that I could carry on with after I finished my amateur and professional skating career. My dad and I, and my business partner, Tim Grech, had been investigating food franchises. After checking out several chains, we finally settled on Cultures Restaurants, which specialize in fresh food.

We liked the youthfulness of the company and the direction it was taking. It wasn't as easy landing a franchise as we thought, but we were finally offered a location in the Don Mills Mall in North York. We just happened to come on the scene at the right time.

It was invigorating learning a new business and it helped to relieve the pressure of skating in a couple of ways. It was something else to concentrate on aside from compulsory figures and triple jumps. And, if my skating fell apart somehow, I would have a safety net. When you're at the top, you have the pressure of having to skate well not only because you want to do your best, but also because you want to make a living from it after your competitive career.

So the 1986-87 season saw my life altered in a number of ways: we had the restaurant, I was working heavily with Peter, I was into rolfing and a new diet, and was still seeking the World title.

I had decided I still needed some more work in figures. Jimmy Grogan of Blue Jay, California, offered to give me a hand. He had seen my figures in Tokyo and thought he could advise me on some things. He wanted me down there for the whole summer, but I could only afford the time for the final two weeks. His school paid for me to come, and I paid for Uschi to accompany me.

What I learned from Jimmy was very simple, very basic theory. A lot of the theory involved rules of "when": when to move my hands, when to move my free foot. It was designed to make me understand the kind of momentum that results in a steady foot. A lot of times I would have a steady foot, but wouldn't know why. Now I learned what to apply to make it happen. What and when.

Some of the techniques were a little old-fashioned and out of date, but Jimmy suggested I try them, and throw out what didn't feel comfortable. He kept a very open mind about it, which is important to me whenever I work with someone. He just wanted to see me win. He had finished second four straight times at the World championship — and five times at the U.S. nationals — and knew all about that kind of gnawing frustration. He joked that he didn't want me to break his record of consecutive second-place finishes. It was his one claim to fame.

I phoned Jimmy after each competition that year, to let him know how the figures went. We also corresponded through the season. He did me an invaluable service. With the summer training I'd had for half a decade from Karol Divin, I could finally feel my figures becoming as good as anybody's in the world.

All kinds of people were being kind to me that year. For instance, the people at the Cricket Club gave me ice time any time I was in Toronto virtually for free. The manager Michael Furst was extremely cooperative. I worked on my own but had terrific encouragement from the veteran coaches, Ellen Burka, Wally Diestelmeyer, Ozzie Colson and Sheldon Galbraith. They always made a point of coming up to me and saying they were glad I was there. Sheldon, particularly, helped me out every day I was there.

I was feeling a lot of support from people and just wanted to get back into a competition, to knock the monkey of Geneva off my back. Finally, it came time to skate in my only fall event — at Budapest.

To backtrack a little, during the summer I had done a judging seminar in Toronto, presided over by Sonia Bianchetti of Italy, who was head of the ISU technical committee, and often acted as a referee of the men's judging panel. They needed some demonstration skaters and although I didn't feel my figures were ready, I went to the seminar anyway. I didn't do great figures there, but at the conclusion, Sonia sat down and went over everything with me: where to correct, little things that could be done to get extra marks. It was very valuable and I sent her a letter of thanks later that summer.

Sonia was at the fall competition in Budapest, where I finished second in figures to Fernand Fedronic of France. I skated a good short and long to win easily. After each discipline she came up to me and praised my work, saying she just couldn't believe the improvement. It was very discreet, but I could tell that she had been impressed. It was helpful to meet someone like Sonia in the off-season, when she was dressed casually. The next time I saw her, I remembered her as a normal person, not as this formal referee who could scare you the way a school principal does.

That autumn week in Budapest was a pivotal time for me. I had something to prove and I proved it. I skated solidly in the short program and landed both axels in the long.

In Budapest I reached a personal landmark with my first international 6.0 for the short program. Moreover, it came from the Soviet judge. Another breakthrough followed a month or so later at the divisional championships in Barrie when I got my first 5.0 in figures.

That year it was decided to do away with the divisional byes for national medallists, an attempt at increasing the audience appeal of those competitions. I wasn't ready to compete at divisionals, and I just tried to get through the week. But because the event was in Barrie, a lot was expected of me. I did what I was ready to do at that point in my training, but didn't skate a very good long, and fell on the second triple axel.

I took a lot of bad press for that fall. I steeled myself for it, especially considering the results of the previous season. The worst came from the *Barrie Banner*, a little paper which comes out two or three times a week. A reporter wrote that he wouldn't bet his last clam on me.

The media can be a little frustrating. Reporters are frequently uninformed or misinformed. They can be very unfair. There are so few members of media who work regularly on figure skating — in 1983 and 1985, for instance, only three Canadians covered the World championships — that the theme and direction of their articles even the positive ones, are often off-base. In each city where a competition is held, the local media members have to become, or pretend to become, well versed in a sport they don't know and probably don't even like.

There are a few who are really good: I will never turn down an interview with Bev Smith of the *Globe and Mail* because she is fair, understands the sport and never tries a trick question. Ron Wilson of CBC-Radio has been at every major championship. Although he has been hard-hitting about my failures, never offering excuses for me, he has helped me out in dealing with the press and has always been honest and fair. That's what you ask for — honesty and fairness. For the most part Canadian journalists, with the obvious exception of guys like Michael Cosgrove or the *Barrie Banner* writer, have been sympathetic. I've grown to like members of the media. I enjoy talking with them and I think the feeling has been mutual. In the final years of my career, I had become experienced enough to detect writers or electronic-media reporters who'd been assigned to figure skating out of the blue, and I could lead the interview, feeding them information so that they got their stories. The Olympics always brings a lot of distant observers out of the woodwork and molds them into instant experts, but they — and their superficial conclusions — are something you learn to live with.

In the mid-to-late eighties, figure skating has had enormous press. It's an individualistic sport with some dynamic stars: Torvill and Dean; Katarina Witt; Elizabeth Manley. Canada has done well, which has attracted attention. Editors know that there is likely to be a Canadian on the podium, a presumption that can't be made in other sports, and couldn't be made in figure skating for more than twenty years.

Over my final couple of years, the press focused in on everything, including what they called my "entourage." A lot of people had approached me to help. When I accepted, they became part of the team: Jimmer, Ann Hall, Jimmy Grogan, Karol Divin among them. But directly involved at a competition, there was really only myself, Doug, Uschi and most recently, Peter. This was still more than most other skaters had involved, I admit, but I felt comfortable with them.

I was aware that the media, and therefore the Canadian public, was wary of me because I had let them down many times before. Winning my seventh Canadian title at Ottawa was really just a small detour on the road to the World championship.

It was in Cincinnati that I hoped to finally wipe away everyone's doubts.

I arrived late at Cincinnati. It was the first year that skaters were notified in advance of the figures group and I wanted to stay home as long as I could, where there was lots of ice time to work on them.

We pulled into Cincinnati on Friday night, with the figures set for Monday. I knew I had only two days until the competition opened, and I was ready to go. Sometimes in the past, I had burned out in practice at the World site.

I was comfortable with the way I had been training and felt at home in my role of not being expected to win — the United States was, after all, the home of the defending champion — but I was very anxious to get going, as I had been all year.

Each figure seemed to get better, even though I was third in the first figure and fourth in the second. In what was a complete shock to everyone, especially those who had seen figures take me out of so many competitions, I actually won the third figure, the loop, which had always been my best. I did incredible figures, the best I'd ever laid down, even in practice.

That put me third behind Aleksandr and Brian. The draw for skating position in the short program left me skating before both of them. If I had to make a choice, I'd prefer it that way, but it doesn't really matter. I used to detest skating first, but I'd simulated it so many times, and drawn that position in enough competitions, that I was at ease with it.

I was really looking forward to doing my new short program because I felt it was such a great routine. Basically a dance number, the "Sing, Sing, Sing" music was particularly suited to the American audience. And the required combination that year was with the double toe loop. In 1988 it would be a double loop, which is a slightly more difficult jump to do coming off a triple axel and therefore wasn't consistent in practice. But in 1987, I don't think I missed a single triple-axel-double-toe-loop combination.

The short program seems suited to me. In the eight World and Olympic championships after 1982, I was never lower than second in it. I like its power, energy and speed, and the fact that to introduce a significant element of artistry to it, you have to be very creative.

I skated an excellent short. Had I been near the end of the draw, I'm sure there would have been some 6.0s. But that was irrelevant. Brian was second and Aleksandr third, which left us standing as we went in, but in a virtual tie for first. The order of our finish in the freeskate would be the final standings. It was the very first time that I'd been in that clear position heading into a World-championship long program.

I drew to skate first in the freeskate, which was fine. I liked my costume, I liked the program and I was skating before the other guys. I felt prepared.

Skating first, it was necessary to go through the walk-through before the warm-up. I'd already been out and looked at the TV lights, and looked at the audience. I was very, very nervous, but I kept my focus well. Two minutes before the warm-up, I saw the other guys coming out and I met up with them. I just looked at Peter and nodded. My arousal level was perfect.

When you skate first, you're really skating for eleven minutes: five minutes warm-up, about a minute and a half before you start, and four and a half minutes of program. Your mind set actually has to be fixed as you step out for warm-up.

That year, Brian had let everyone know that he was going to try to land the world's first quadruple jump in his program. And, apparently, he landed one during the warm-up. I didn't see it, didn't know he'd done it, and didn't hear the crowd cheer when he did it. I did hear them yell when I did the triple-axel combination, and that indicates a good, positive psychological state. I know that I did do the first axel in practice, a personal goal.

I came off with a minute to go in the six-minute warm-up, and that sixty seconds just flew by. I had time to sit down for ten seconds and collect myself. I never had a thought about how close I was to being World champion, or about the failure in Geneva. Switzerland had been wiped out of my mind by a good performance in Budapest.

After walking through the program to the first jump, the triple Lutz, I heard them announce, "Skaters, please clear the ice." I had about fifteen seconds at that point, I took off my skate guards and went onto the ice. Everything seemed normal.

I did a nice Lutz to start, then landed the triple-axel-double-toe-loop combination. Bingo. I knew I was fine. I did a solid triple flip in the slow section, then it was clear sailing. Near the end of the program, I approached the second triple axel.

I was feeling good, digging deep for the expressiveness I knew I would need to gain a few extra marks, and then I focused on that axel. There isn't much of a lead-in and when I came down successfully, the crowd cheered again. It was the first time in World-championship history that *two* triple axels had ever been successfully landed in the same program.

I was concentrating so much on that second axel that I had almost nothing left. A wave of fatigue swept over me and I told myself not to do something silly. I was scheduled to end with a double flip, and a couple of hops leading directly into a triple toe loop. As I came down from the flip onto my right foot, I decided to do only a double toe loop, just to be careful.

By this point, anyway, people were starting to stand up. I couldn't see them, but I could feel them, sense the energy.

When I came off, I felt great about my performance. It couldn't have been much better. There was the double toe loop, but the rest of the tricks easily made up for it. But there was no feeling of, "I've done it," because Aleksandr and Brian, both World champions, were yet to skate.

Uschi, Doug and Peter were beaming. We had done our jobs. The performance was of World-championship caliber, there were two triple axels, it was very expressive and we got good marks. It was now out of our hands.

With the other two contenders yet to skate, I wanted to find a television monitor, so Steve Milton led Doug and me into the press area where many of the Canadian media were gathered to watch the results. Uschi was too emotional to watch the other two skaters and left the building.

Aleksandr, who had a sore groin muscle, took himself out of it early by falling on his triple axel. Then it was Brian's turn. His quadruple jump, which takes a long time to set up, was scheduled for early in the program and when the music built up to it, I put my hands over my face and said, "I don't think I can watch this." But I opened my fingers and peered through them at the screen as Brian tried to become the first in the world to land the quad. His skate slipped from under him and he missed. I didn't feel any relief. Brian continued his program and made some other mistakes, stumbling on his flip and doubling another triple.

As he finished and waited for his marks, my heart was racing as it had been since I finished my performance. Deep down I felt that I had won, but I didn't want to show anything in case I was wrong.

After his marks came up, the standing on the monitor began to scramble to include Brian's.

It seemed to take forever, but when the blips on the screen were still, it showed Brian Orser at the top.

I was World champion.

The CBS and CBC cameras were rolling, and watching the replays, I see that I jumped in the air, grabbed Doug and then hugged a couple of reporters and CFSA people who had been with me for such a long time.

I don't really remember doing that. But I do recall saying, almost calmly, "I did it." That wasn't so much of a hurrah, but rather a realization that it had finally happened. I was the best in the world. Period. Amen.

After Doug and I hugged we pulled back and looked at each other. There were no words, but this was our way of communicating. It always has been. Words can sometimes mess things up with both of us. But there was no mistaking this feeling, this recognition of what we had done. It was so appropriate that Doug would be standing right beside me at the exact instant I became World champion. This was something we both had earned. He didn't just coach me, he had been there from Day One. Working out of rural Ontario, he had guided a World champion from the very beginning to the very end.

Initially, the experience wasn't what I had expected. I never really knew how I'd react. For years, I had visualized becoming World champion, and had imagined oceans of hugging and crying and a heavy release of emotions. But after the first realization, things became very calm. I had things to do, too.

I did a couple of interviews, found Uschi, who had come back in, and then I finally saw my family. My mother was crying, of course. We all hugged, and enjoyed the moment, but I was surprisingly calm and under control.

Until it came time for the medal presentation.

Waiting at the edge of the boards, my chest was tight and pounding. When the announcement came over the arena speakers ". . . World champion" my breath got a little short and my skin started to tingle. By the time he said, ". . . Bri-an . . . Or-ser" the crowd was on its feet. I went out to take my bow and then it all hit me and I started to get choked up. I bit my lip because I figured once I started to show my emotion, there would be no way of stopping it.

To add even a little more drama, I purposely stepped onto the silver-medallist's platform — where I had had to stop so many times before — hesitated, and took an exaggerated step onto the top of the podium. Sort of a "giant step for mankind." The crowd roared even more.

As I stood in the gold-medallist's spot, I looked around and surveyed the territory, thinking back to all the frustrations of previous years. They announced Brian Boitano. I applauded his appearance, and we congratulated each other. We are close friends, but I didn't really feel sorry for him, because he had already won the World championship, the one I had lost. I had been second so many times that, although I never gloated over this, I did enjoy a little selfish pleasure in relishing a moment I felt I deserved. Then Aleksandr came out to receive his third bronze medal of World competition.

When I won fall internationals, and they played "O Canada," I loved that proud feeling of representing Canada, but I fantasized about the anthem playing at the World championship. Now it was finally happening and it was not at all the same as a fall competition. There was the Canadian flag sliding up the pole first, followed by the flags of the two most powerful nations in the world on either side, and slightly lower. It was very moving symbolism.

At that moment, I had a sense of representing every skater in Canada, competitive and recreational. I wasn't Brian Orser, best in the world; it was *Canada*, best in the world.

When they reached the final few bars of the national anthem — the last "O Canada" — I couldn't contain it any longer and the tears started rolling down my cheeks. CBS-TV zoomed in for the shot and beamed it around the world.

Then we stepped off the podium, skated around the arena, waving to the crowd, and off the ice.

My sister, Mary Kay, accompanied me to the doping room where we had a beer and relaxed. We were both feeling a little humbled and overwhelmed by it all. It was a chance to escape for a few moments and we sat back and said, "Holy cow." There was so much excitement outside, and it was so calm inside. We didn't say too much. Mary Kay and I had started skating together when we were little more than toddlers and inside this room we had a chance to privately share our pride about what had happened.

During the press conference that followed, Brian and I sat close to each other. He said that he wasn't feeling as bad as he had thought he might, that he would become a better person because of it, and that he was looking forward to the Olympics. Because we're good friends, I was relieved that he didn't feel bad and I wasn't worried about him. We both agreed that the missed quad was not the difference on this night.

We hadn't been presented with our actual medals, because there had been a mix-up and the wrong boxes were sent over from the ISU headquarters. Instead, we got smaller, ISU figures medals. The real medals didn't come until the next day, but I didn't care. My medals and trophies are actually insignificant. We still have them all, but a lot of the World medals and coins are in a Loblaws shopping bag in my mother's closet. I have a small trophy shelf at home, but it's full of a lot of things from younger years: the picture of Donald Jackson, two of my casts, the certificate from the Canada Games, and a lot of people pictures. It's the people who were important, not the medals. I'll probably display them sometime in the future, but for now I carry all the memories in my mind.

I had some time alone with those memories when I went back to the hotel to change for the party. When I went into the room, I wanted to kick my heels for joy, but what I did was look into the mirror and give myself a big smile and a pat on the back. It was a great moment, just on my own.

Then I phoned Marilyn Symko, Gordon Forbes's coach. I liked Gordon so much and I liked her because she had helped Gordon. She had been a part of this thing since 1981 and had always been very supportive and a great confidante. She was on the phone with Gordon and when she got off all I did was repeat one of her favorite phrases — "Now THAT's the ticket" — and we had a huge laugh together. I was so excited that I wanted to reach out and touch someone who wasn't there to share it with and I thought she would be the one who got the greatest kick out of it.

There was a celebration planned at another hotel and, heading toward it, Doug and I ran into each other in the lobby. As we walked to the party, we both ran into Scott Hamilton. "Your prices just went up," he said to Doug and laughed. Scott had interviewed me for CBS. He had immediately mentioned the significance of my hesitation on the silver-medal step. It was a light-hearted interview. Scott had always wanted me to win the World title, and he was enjoying my success.

There were hundreds and hundreds of people at the party. I ran into Johnny Esaw and said, "I wish it was you out there, Johnny." I had nothing against the CBC, but CTV had been such a big part of my career, and figure skating to that point. I heard that even Toller Cranston had told Johnny that, by rights, it should have been him.

That party was a like a collage of my life: my family, lots of skating friends, coaches, CFSA officials, judges, media people, and government officials.

These people had waited so long for me to win a World championship that I thought I owed it to them in a certain way. I'd always known that I was one of the world's top skaters, but I didn't have the right medal. Until that night, it always scared me that I didn't have a World title and that I might never get one. But now, no one could take it away. That's one of the things that got me through a tough period the next year.

When I ran into government people, I almost felt like I was saying, "There you go." The Best Ever program is the biggest thing that has ever happened to Canadian sports, although it lays an incredible amount of pressure on the individual athletes to produce. I felt satisfaction in delivering, and felt good for the CFSA, who had supported me so long and who had to answer to their government sponsors, too.

So, on the night that I became World champion, my primary emotion was actually one of relief.

The champagne flowed and there were short speeches by my dad, Otto Jelinek (who was then federal minister for sports) and Doug. I also spoke briefly, but none of us wanted to formalize the proceedings. We all just wanted to enjoy it and feel it.

Because it was so noisy, the party was broken up by hotel security police. My family and the Simpson family adjourned to my brother's room for a private party. Doug and Michelle were there and we had a little toast to all of us, recognizing how far we had all come from Midland, Penetang, Elmvale and Orillia. Dad toasted Larry and Lou Simpson for being with us right from the start, and mentioned Michelle and I growing up together. We all shed a few tears, had a toast and drank more champagne.

And that was it.

After the dance and ladies' events finished, we did the exhibitions and for the first time, I got to skate in the final four. That's the spot reserved strictly for World champions.

6. The Battle of the Brians

I have always stated publicly that my skating was for Brian Orser and for no one else. This was partly to avoid self-inflicted pressure. In reality, I have also skated for Canada.

I am very proud to be a Canadian and I love everything about this country. Whenever we travelled through Europe, there was a special feeling on the day the tour ended, that sense of getting back. Not just home, but to Canada.

In Europe, Asia and the United States, I am acutely aware that I represent my country. When I first started skating internationally, it was never, "Did you see Brian Orser's triple axel?" but, "Did you see the *Canadian's* triple axel?" I was very proud of that label.

Growing in rural Ontario, in the midst of the snow, and living on the edge of a lake all of my life, I must have been seen as the quintessential Canadian by skaters from other countries. People associate snow and big lakes with Canada.

There are a lot of things that distinguish Canada from other countries: the weather, distances, a sense of fairness and most of all, I think, the fact that we are a humble people. Not naive; humble. I love that national characteristic and have tried hard to live up to it.

So, I was bursting with emotion when the ISU tour made its second 1987 stop at Toronto. It strikes me that of all the players on that Midland novice hockey team so many years ago, I was probably the only one who never dreamed of performing in front of a huge crowd at Maple Leaf Gardens. Yet, I was the only one who made it.

The city of Orillia had arranged to make a presentation the night the tour hit the Gardens. As Geoff Hewitt, one of the city councillors, waited at center ice before the show, I came out by the boards, wearing my World-team jacket. They hadn't even announced my name, but the spotlight found me and people began standing up. The Gardens was packed and, as more and more people noticed me, the roar grew deafening. I looked up in shock, gazing all around the stands. I'd skated in front of big crowds before, but suddenly I felt a huge lump in my throat. I hadn't been expecting so much emotion from the fans, and I was overwhelmed. There was so much support there, 17,000 Canadians leaping to their feet clapping and thanking me. Once again I felt a surge of relief for finally rewarding people for their long wait. It was one of the greatest nights of my career. At that moment I experienced a deeper understanding of what it meant to be World champion.

I was scheduled to skate last on the program and wanted to perform well, which I did. It was a perfect evening.

Later that night, I stuck my hand in an elevator door, trying to prevent it from closing. Early in the morning the hand was throbbing so much that I went to the hospital for x-rays. I had broken my hand, and had to wear a small cast.

The show has to go on, so I was back out there that night, doing back-flips with a cast on. The first couple of nights, flinging my arm around in the jumps really hurt the hand. With four cities to go on the tour, I visited some doctors in Los Angeles, who felt that I should have pins put in the hand. I skipped the final bit of the tour and went home, checked with team physicians and they decided against pins. They just put a bigger cast on it.

No one knew I was home, so I just hid out and worked in the restaurant. I really enjoyed that. There were dozens of times at work or in the car when I'd suddenly have a great feeling wash over me, a sense that I was World champion. It wasn't the adoration or attention that I enjoyed most, but those private moments of satisfaction.

One other long-awaited piece of business had to be attended to. I went to John Knebli and, as he had promised three years earlier, he showed me where the gold was stitched into my skating boots. I didn't take it out, though, and the boots are serving as display bookends now.

The city of Orillia had a mammoth celebration for me that spring — a parade and a big reception that went on until after one in the morning. I had prepared something special for the occasion. For each member of my family and for my coaches I had ordered replicas of the gold medal they had all helped me to win. At the reception I gave them out, with a little capsule comment of what each person had meant to me. I gave them to my mother and father; my grandparents; Janice and her husband, Tom; Bob and his wife, Sheri; Michael and his wife, Denise; Mary Kay and her husband, Joe; Uschi; and Doug. Later I also gave one to my aunt Kathy. When she died, the medal went to her good friend, Jimmer. So Kathy lived on with us in spirit.

There was a two-week vacation scheduled for Malta in May, but just before I went, I found my music for the 1988 season, which would be my last amateur year.

I had heard this music before. Dennis Coi had used it when he was still an amateur, but no one knew the name of the piece. Uschi played music for me over the phone, but we couldn't find it. Finally, I phoned Ellen Burka and she thought she knew what it was. I went to Toronto and sat in her living room and with the very first beat of the music, I knew that was it — "The Bolt" by Shostakovich.

I called Uschi right away and said I had found it. She had already cut a whole program for me, as insurance, but I still haven't heard it because, for years, I had wanted to skate to "The Bolt."

Just before my holiday, I went to Port Coquitlam, British Columbia, for Tracy Wilson's wedding. It was a wonderful time. While we were there, Rob McCall and I went to visit Dennis Coi in nearby Vancouver. Dennis, who had won a national bronze medal in 1982, was dying of AIDS. It was very difficult seeing him. I had never lost a friend, someone close to my age, and this was a very rough time. But I knew that Dennis was dying, and I didn't want him to hear the music and think that I had stolen it from him. He was ecstatic that I was going to skate to "The Bolt," and said that it was his favorite piece of music. Dennis made us feel very relaxed and even cracked a few jokes. The skating world lost a great personality when he died a couple of months later.

After my vacation, I came back refreshed and ready to tackle 1988, which I knew was going to be a pressure-filled year with the Olympics in Calgary. It was the earliest that the music for both the long ("The Bolt") and short ("Sing, Sing, Sing" again) had ever been set and I could go right into working out the program during the first week of practice.

I played the music at least three times every session, compared to the normal once. And, in contrast to other years, when I worried what people would think of the music, I knew they had to like this because I liked it so much. The music was in my head all the time.

During the late summer, I came very close to working with the brilliant dancer/choreographer Mikhail Baryshnikov.

Uschi knew how I admired his work and was determined we would get together. Through a friend, twice it appeared we would work together but it fell through each time.

It developed that for the first time I choreographed my own program. This was gratifying to Uschi, because it followed her "game plan" of having me graduate to the point of putting my own routine together. She pointed me in the right direction a couple of times, and I would pick it up from there. The last, and most difficult, segment to choreograph was the opening stance. I wanted to show the power and intensity of the music, but didn't want to appear haughty, so it had to have some subtlety.

In preparation for the Olympics, representatives of the media were starting to pour into Orillia in a steady flow that summer. Doug did some pretty fancy choreography himself, balancing my need for intense practice and the media's need to get their stories. He did the job well, but I know that several times that fall he had to get tough and refuse interviews. He even turned down *Time* magazine, which wanted to do a photo session at an inappropriate time.

There was another distraction. Doug had started to have some problems with the city administration. The summer before, they had approved the idea for a new rink, which would be designed to accommodate figure skating and the junior A hockey team. Then council reversed its decision, and voted to sink more money into the Community Centre, which had been closed because it had failed some safety tests. The plan for a new rink was scrapped. That was the start of it. Doug entered into preliminary negotiations with the City of Barrie for a new rink. It was a complicated political scene. Doug did move the school to Barrie at the end of 1988, but the upshot was that it became a bitter situation. It didn't have much effect on my training, but it was frustrating to see Doug get angry and hurt. There were some problems with ice time. More than once, we were told it was only available late at night, then found out that it had been empty earlier. And there were problems with the quality of the ice. Brian Orser Arena had always had perfect ice for figure skating. They always took tremendous pride in the surface. Figure-skating ice needs to be softer than hockey ice, so you can get a good grip taking off and landing, and so that it cushions the impact. Yet it also needs to be fast, which is tough to do while keeping it soft. Orillia did it. They also maintained an even color on the surface, and despite problems with heaving cement, managed to keep the ice level. In that final year, however, the color was splotchy and there were all kinds of small hills on the ice. I think they might have stopped caring so much because they knew Mariposa was leaving. Later, the city hosted a reception to honor people in the area going to the Olympics and all of us, including some kind of dance troupe, which was part of the ceremonies, were given awards. All except Doug. The explanation was that, as a coach, he wasn't an "official" Olympian, but so what? It was a cruel thing to do.

By mid-fall I started to notice the build-up of the "Battle of the Brians." Both of us were scheduled to skate at Skate Canada in Calgary and there was an awful lot of press comment about Brian having hired Sandra Bezic, the Canadian choreographer who had worked with Barb and Paul. Sandra and I had always been very close and I knew that she was very talented. I knew she could make a difference with Brian, and make my job more difficult, but I didn't hold it against her. Skating is a business.

Brian wasn't going to try the quad at the Olympics. He was adding a second triple axel and was becoming more artistic, skating to a military theme — "Napoleon". We both skated poorly in the short program at Skate Canada, missing our triple-axel-double-loop combinations. But in the long, we both skated quite well. He skated before I did and turned in a good performance. I followed and also skated fairly well, winning five of the seven judges and the gold medal.

I felt I hadn't skated anywhere near my potential, but at the press conference, Brian said he would have accepted his performance at the Olympics. As it turned out, he skated much, much better in Calgary three months later.

The Battle of the Brians added a great deal of pressure to Skate Canada and that pressure and hype multiplied a hundredfold over the next few months. I kept reading about Brian's artistic programs, but I couldn't get it through people's heads that I had just beaten him over all, *and* in artistic impression.

In mid-season, I started having some problems in training and decided to seek the help of Peter Jensen's wife, Sandra, who is a psychologist. By December, the Olympics were plastered everywhere — on the newsstands, TV, billboards, milk cartons, cereal boxes. It was a vise of pressure and it started affecting me in practice. I'd always vented frustration in training, but the frustration had never been like this. I wanted to do so well for Canada. When I didn't train well, I'd totally lose control, kicking the boards over and over and over again, my body shaking in anger. Sometimes I'd walk right out of the practice.

I had three sessions with Sandra and she helped me to relive that feeling of anger. I told her it was like another person coming out. I had got to the point where I was actually talking to this other person. We decided that this was actually the "strength" of me, coming out to protect me against pressure and bad situations.

I know this sounds like Sybil, but apparently most people have these other personalities. Sandra told me this was entirely normal, especially in my stressful situation, and we devised a strategy in which I'd bring this other personality out in the car on the way to the rink. I'd bring him out and let him know he was out, so he didn't have to smash his way out. I guess you could compare this personality to a dumb bodyguard. Not much intelligence, only strength and emotion. In any case, I never had another outburst after that.

I felt uncomfortable about this other personality — not with myself, because it developed into a good thing, but in telling people about it. In the end, it became a joke with those close to me. I told Rob McCall about it. One day, he, Liz Manley and I were in a car, and there was a noise. Rob asked me if I said something, and I hadn't. He asked Liz, and she said she hadn't said anything. Then he looked back at me and said, "Maybe it was that *other* guy."

We all broke up.

After the fact, we could laugh about it, but I was very scared going through this. After the first session with Sandra, I was so wiped out, I couldn't get out of bed for a day. I later realized it was all part of dealing with the Olympics.

Before the Olympics, I still had to deal with nationals. It would be my last appearance at the Canadians competition. I came into Victoria, won the figures — although I didn't skate well and needed to win the loop to pull ahead of Neil Paterson — and still I carried a mental block about missing the combination. That was put to rest in the short program when I landed it perfectly. The crowd went crazy as I finished and went completely wild when the marks came up. All seven judges gave me 5.9 for technical merit and every single judge gave me a perfect 6.0 for artistic impression.

The long was a total disaster. In my walkthrough I seemed to be doing everything right. I wasn't as nervous as I should have been, however, and next thing I knew I was sitting on my butt on the ice. I missed both axels and doubled the flip and the loop. It was a nightmare all around.

Runner-up Kurt Browning didn't skate his best, so I won my eighth and final national championship, but it wasn't the way I wanted to go out. I read a lot of bad press and everyone was very concerned, but I dealt with that real easily. I said to myself, "Just wait." In 1984, I had skated poorly in Regina, but had gone on to win both the short and long programs at the Olympics. I wasn't worried about my performance at Canadians.

I did start to become a little afraid of going to Calgary. That was an inappropriate feeling, but if you were to talk to all the other athletes, I'm sure you'd discover a similar fear. The only residue from Victoria was that if it happened again at Calgary, it would be a disaster. It would crush me as a skater and would crush my professional career.

However, I was skating well, so the self-doubt wasn't overwhelming. And I was getting hundreds, thousands, of letters and cards from Canadians. Most of them were from school kids and many were projects on the Olympics. I wasn't that long out of school myself and could still remember doing projects on people like John F. Kennedy. Now I was the subject of projects.

The media onslaught was really concentrated by now, but we had a handle on that. Almost a year previously, we had anticipated this kind of attention and, thanks to Doug, we were well-prepared for it. He blocked a lot of interviews, kept others short and, when I was skating, I could bounce frustration off him.

There was no escaping the Olympic hype, though. Even if I hadn't seen it everywhere — seen my picture and Brian's on the front of every magazine — I would have it in my mind, anyway. I had spent a lot of time visualizing the night of the long program to help ease into the pressure. The way I looked at it, the more I saw myself on TV (which I don't watch often) and in print, the better. It was very different than Sarajevo. The hype was a hundred times more intense.

I was skating well, practicing normally, and on my final day in Barrie, I did perfect programs. The whole thing wasn't as dramatic as I thought it would be because I was ready for it.

We were aware of the pressure over the final three months, especially as I was Canada's only reigning World champion heading into Calgary, but I wasn't buckling. I just dealt with it as it came along. We made it a gradual build-up with no surprises.

We arrived in Calgary on Friday, February 12, and the feeling was electric. All the athletes were hyper, running around the corridors of the athletes' village, bursting with nervous energy. That night there was a reception for the Canadian delegation where they would announce who would carry Canada's flag into McMahon Stadium during the opening ceremonies. Part-way through the reception, Roger Jackson, head of the Canadian Olympic Committee, took the podium for a speech. Near the end he said, "I'm proud to announce that the athlete chosen is" and then, for effect, he paused for what seemed like hours ". . . Brian Orser."

The room broke into cheers and I got all choked up. Luckily, I had a few moments to get myself together while Roger finished his speech and I shook a few hands. Andy Shaw, who runs the public-relations firm where Teresa Moore (who would be my media liaison through the Olympics) now works, had prepared a little bilingual speech for me. He had anticipated that I would be chosen.

My parents were both crying, and it was warming that the other Canadian athletes were supportive of the decision. After my speech I went out to meet the press, although there wasn't much to say — just how proud I was.

The next day we assembled in the village courtyard. It was a spectacular sight, all the different styles and colors of outfits. Our uniforms were being kept secret until the very end. Finally we were shown our red parade coats, with the white fringe and the white cowboy hats. There were some complaints that we'd never be able to wear those coats again because they were so flashy, but all of us have coats from other years. When we got together with the other teams, ours stood out brilliantly.

In the marshaling area, at Father David Bauer Arena, the athletes sat in the stands, by country, waiting for the cue to start marching out. Suddenly, the Canadian team started doing the "wave." Other countries picked it up and it would travel around the arena until it got to the Soviets, where it would stop. Then, we'd start it again: a mounting wave, lots of cheering, through the Americans who were seated next to the Soviets, and then it screeched to an abrupt stop again. The only Russian who caught it was Vladimir Kotin, their free spirit.

Finally, the third time, the Soviet team got the message and when the wave reached them they all jumped up and yelled. You could see on their faces the recognition of what this was about and how much they enjoyed it. When they stood up, the place went completely wild, everyone cheering, clapping, yelling. What a jolting experience! The only people there were athletes — the world's best young winter sportspeople — and it was a physical show of unity.

Greece, the founding country of the Olympics, was first into the stadium and we were last, following Yugoslavia. As we waited, you could hear the roars from the 50,000 people as the athletes from each country appeared in McMahon Stadium. As we marched along the quarter-mile to the stadium from the arena, people without tickets were lined up cheering us and waving flags. It was incredible.

Yugoslavia went in and got a big ovation. We were next, but they held us back so we couldn't be seen. We paraded through the tunnel under the stands and even before they announced CAN-A-DA people began to catch sight of our red coats. They were just waiting for us, and to be the first one through the tunnel was a very heavy experience. There was a fierce Canadian pride in Calgary, and when I stepped out with the flag, the reception was thunderous. As we passed each section of the stands, the ovation kept getting louder and louder. It's impossible to describe how moving that parade was and how *Canadian* I felt.

The opening ceremonies were on a Saturday, and on Wednesday morning our competition began with the figures. I had a good draw, skating near the end for the first figure, and near the beginning for the loop. I was nervous, but had had a good sleep the night before. I walked over with Peter to discover that the event had been delayed because Ben Wright, the referee, had taken sick and Donald Gilchrist, a Canadian, took over. My first figure was average, but the double-three was one of my best ever and I stood third. I had some time to kill before the loop so we walked over by McMahon Stadium and looked at the flame. I came back to the rink and did a good loop. Not my best loop, but it kept me third.

Fadeev was first, Boitano second. That set the table for the two freestyle events. The short program was on the following night in the Calgary Corral. I felt a great deal of pressure lifted, now that figures were over. I was thrilled to be third.

I skated first in the final group for the short program and Brian was fourth. With one minute to go, I came off the ice and Paul Martini, who was working with one of the television networks, opened a door for me, so I didn't have to go off the ice the normal way and make a long walk around to the starting door. I did my walk through to the first jump and it was my turn to skate.

I was nervous, but anxious to do it. When it was my turn, I gave Doug my skate guards, we exchanged signals and I went out to perform. It was the first time I had actually been presented to the audience and the huge ovation psyched me up. I whipped through the program cleanly with lots of feeling, landed the combination halfway through and sailed home. Considering the pressure, the difficulty of that particular combination and that everyone in front of me had skated cleanly so there was no room for error, it was my best short program. When I finished, even though there were five others to skate, I knew I had won it.

I watched the monitor as Brian skated. He performed very well, and finished second. That left him first over all with 2.0 points and me second with 2.2. Just as twelve months of hype had predicted, whoever won the long program would be Olympic champion.

Brian drew to skate first in the final group for the long program and I skated third. Being honest, I would rather have skated first, but I had skated after him at Skate Canada and won, so I wasn't overly concerned. For the moment, I was happy with my short program. The short is a do-or-die test: it can't help you much, but it can kill you if you don't do well.

There was a day off before the freeskate and the media was beginning to get really pushy. They wanted to spend so much time with me that I just couldn't spare. I needed to concentrate. Luckily, at the Olympics, you can just hide out in the village. When I wasn't practicing, I did exactly that. I waited in the Olympic Village for the four and a half minutes that would culminate the Battle of the Brians, the most widely discussed and anticipated individual confrontation of these Olympics.

The morning of Saturday, February 20, dawned sunny and very warm. It was just like spring, which played havoc with skiing events, but it injected many of us with a stirring of hope.

I had gone to bed late the night before. My practice on the day of the long program was scheduled for 1:00 P.M., and I didn't want to get up too early just to sit around and wait.

I got out of bed about 10:00 A.M. and didn't feel nervous at all. Even when I thought about what lay ahead, I didn't get any butterflies . . . . In fact, all day I had a pretty good feeling.

I had a good practice, although I didn't try everything. But I did land the triple flip, which seemed like a good omen. After the practice, I came back to the athletes' village and listened to *Swan Lake* on my Walkman, then began my ritual of packing.

On the day of the long program, I always pack my suitcase. It's productive . . . and it passes time. I tucked away my scribe, my short-program costume and all the clothes that I wouldn't be wearing before the end of the Olympics the next weekend. The packing took me through to about four o'clock in the afternoon. Rob McCall, my roommate, was in and out most of the afternoon and we talked casually. Then I worked with Jimmer in the village's medical room. It was more of a massage than a rolfing session and lasted about an hour.

By now it was 5:30 and, over at the Saddledome, the men's long program of the xvth Olympics had already begun.

I didn't have to leave until 6:30 P.M. so I went upstairs and made my power shake. Then I went for my precompetition walk. I strolled out of the village and over to the flame at McMahon Stadium. I wasn't nervous but I was very anxious, almost hyper, to get it done. I used the walk to suck in a good supply of fresh air.

I chose a route that included the stadium because it was so inspiring. This was what the last four years had all been leading up to. The sun was just beginning to set and in the fading light, the flame seemed to be burning even brighter. Gazing at it was very moving. I just let it flow over me, and didn't think about anything.

After about thirty minutes, I came back into the village and transferred some things to another, unoccupied room, because Rob started his competition the next day and I didn't want to come back after my event and disturb his sleep. I got my costume and skates together. As I usually do, I took a look at myself in the mirror to get pumped up and get in touch with myself. Usually I see somebody confident, and I did this time too. I took one last look around the room and quickly thought to myself, "I'll be coming back as Olympic champion."

Uschi, Peter and I travelled over to the Saddledome in a Games van. We didn't say much, although Uschi started talking until I told her it was making me a bit nervous. We got out of the van and ran smack into the cameras, dozens of them . . . . it didn't bother me because I felt confident. They had been following me everywhere all week — all year, really.

By now I was focused entirely on my program. As I entered the building I hummed my music over and over. I went through some moves even as I walked in. I sort of skipped through certain parts. I walked through the triple flip several times, because it's the one jump I could have problems with. It's a high-risk jump for me, but usually came off in the program when it counted.

I saw Brian Boitano when I came in, and he was pretty intense. He was a few minutes ahead of me in preparation because he was skating first and I was third. We talked a little bit about how excited we were that we'd both be finished tonight.

I walked around in my sweatsuit. When the second last group of skaters was warming up I went out by the ice surface to get in touch with it. It was a necessary step because the ice surface offers such a dramatic change, with all the bright lights overhead, and the 20,000 people in the audience. A few hundred fans noticed me and started cheering, but I felt totally in control. Somebody tried to tell me where my parents were sitting, but I told him not to.

I came back into the hallway under the stands and finished getting warmed up — the cameras on me, as they had been on Brian — while Doug, Uschi and Peter watched silently. Some of the other athletes, including the pairs skaters, were there. I guess I most recall Denise Benning. Earlier in the week, I'd had a very bad practice. Peter came and got me, and he and I and Denise had a session in this little library in the village.

Peter wanted me to talk to Denise. She blurted out that she was scared to death and started to cry. I tried to talk to her and tell her that it was good to be afraid, of course you'll have fear, and that I was afraid because I was doing my figures the next day. We talked for at least an hour. She wasn't skating consistently, but I gave her a few examples — Barb and Paul, for instance — of consistent skaters who didn't always win. I could see in her eyes that the talk had made a difference. The next night she went out and skated well to finish sixth.

After that walkthrough I went in to the dressing room and got into my costume.

I went into the washroom to put on some make-up and one other skater was in there doing the same thing: Brian Boitano.

It was just Brian and me. The room suddenly seemed incredibly quiet and very, very intense. It crossed my mind several times that this was *the Olympics*, that it was the Big Time. There had been several occasions during the week when I'd thought of that. I had learned not to shut such realizations out.

I put on my skates and went out to the ice. My warm-up was very low-key and very relaxed. I didn't come out like gangbusters at all. I came close to Brian one time and was cut off once by Grzegorz Filipowski. Nothing was going to stop me at that time, except Filipowski, who is normally very difficult during a warm-up.

I came off the ice and by now the ball was rolling. I put my skate guards on. They announced Brian's name and moments later I heard the first strains of "Napoleon." I started walking through my program with Doug and Uschi and Peter watching. I was listening to the audience a little bit. Because of what had happened in Geneva, I wasn't going to avoid it. Walking through my program took me through his, so we finished at the same time. I heard the marks and I told Peter and Doug that they'd left room. "They didn't leave a lot though," I said, and I knew I had to be good and do everything. I knew from the marks and the crowd noise that he hadn't missed anything.

Aleksandr was next and I didn't pay attention at all because I knew he was out of it. I went through my first two jumps again while Aleksandr was skating.

I went onto the ice as he took his bow and collected the flowers. That's usually the absolute worst time, but I felt good. Then, when they called my name, the Saddledome went wild. I just wanted to perform for them and what I said to myself was, "Just watch me go."

The music began and I started.

The Lutz was first. Looking over my shoulder, I went into it. It felt really good, one of the very best I'd ever done. It's always good to have the first jump out of the way, because it tends to set the tone for the program. Next was the triple-axel combination. I was a little apprehensive. I was afraid of it because I'd missed it a few times in practice and had missed it at Canadians. But it went really well. Extremely well, in fact, and I was buoyed with confidence.

The steps after the combination went well, as did a little portion of footwork where I play up to the judges. They seemed to be smiling — I think, on the whole, they were hoping that I would skate well enough to win. I was feeling loose as I moved down toward Doug and Uschi and it was triple-flip time.

I felt good going into the jump, but in the air I knew that something was wrong. I instantly thought that the only saving grace would be to stay on feet. My protective instincts took over and I stepped out of the jump and made sure that I kept skating, trying to cover up the error. I didn't think at all that I'd blown the gold medal, because I didn't make a big thing of it. I went right into a triple-Salchow-double-loop combination, which was bang-on. I thought I had camouflaged as well I could. It was one little mistake which could be overlooked.

Then I went into the flying camel spin, which I do on a forward inside edge for a little variety and that was the end of the first section of the music.

I was now into the slow section, which I knew I had to milk for extra marks. My thinking now was that the decision would probably come down to artistic merit. I went into the triple-loop jump, which came off well, and then into another fast portion. There was footwork, a jump series with a double axel, a couple of hops and a triple toe loop, and the audience reacted with a roar. The second slow portion followed with a lot of descriptive moves aimed at the judges. Those eventually would lead me on to the second triple axel.

After the jump sequence, I came out of a spin and noticed that I was a little tired. While moving toward the axel, I concluded that I had to stay on my feet, that I couldn't afford a fall. About ten seconds before the jump I made the decision, which, with the benefit of 20-20 hindsight, probably cost Canada its only gold medal of the Games. I would only do a double axel.

Although I knew that Brian Boitano had skated very well and had good technical marks, I didn't know if he had done *his* second triple axel. Remember that the previous year, when I did two in one program, it was the first time that it had ever been accomplished. Had I known that he made his second axel — or appeared to, since replays showed a flaw — I might have tried my second axel. But maybe I would have fallen. In fact, I'm pretty sure I wouldn't have landed it. If I had attempted it, fallen, and *that* had cost me the gold, it would have been Geneva all over again.

So I did a good double axel and got something of a second wind. I went into a series of split jumps and felt pretty good. That ending was similar to the one in Cincinnati. The jumps felt much crispier, although the last triple toe loop was a bit small. But in Cincinnati, I doubled that toe loop, and the split jumps were much lower. But because I won there, and lost in Calgary, people thought I didn't finish as strongly. Perspective can color a lot of opinions.

My first reaction when I finished was that I'd done it. I'd stayed on my feet, the program was relatively clean and the audience liked it.

I thought I had won.

That's why I didn't pick up any of my flowers or linger on the ice too long. I thought the sooner I got off, the sooner the marks would come up. When the first set flashed up I thought, "Oooh, oohh." They were all 5.8s except the mark awarded by the Czechoslovakian judge, Gerhardt Bubnik, who gave me 5.9. I knew Brian had had a lot of 5.8s too, but I didn't know exactly how many.

The artistic-impression marks came up and there were five 5.9s, three 5.8s and a perfect 6.0 from the Czech judge. My heart leapt and I thought, "Yes, I've done it." I couldn't stop looking at the 6.0. It was the first I'd ever had in competition at this level.

I quickly searched out Brian Pockar and Debbie Wilkes at the broadcast booth. I could see them madly switching television monitor channels to find the ranking on the computer. Then I saw the expression on their faces sag and I thought, "Oh, no." Then another man looked over at me and reluctantly held up two fingers.

Then I knew.

Immediately, a whole range of emotions battered me and it was difficult to sort them all out. The disappointment cut like a knife, ripped through every part of me. It was beyond any sense of loss that I'd ever felt before. I was also a little bit annoyed with the judging panel. I thought, "How can they do this to me?" Then I was thinking, "Why didn't they do it four years ago when they should have?"

And this was the most surprising emotion of all: Suddenly I

became very angry that I hadn't won in 1984. In Sarajevo, and in all the time since, not winning the 1984 Olympics didn't bother me anything like as much as it did in sixty seconds after the 1988 Olympics. I'd been living through four years of skating just to get this title that I felt I deserved four years ago. I knew in 1984 that I would come back four years later and win it. When it didn't happen, I thought, "How can they do this to me? Haven't they noticed the incredible pressure I've been under? Haven't they read that I'm Canada's only hope for a gold medal in these games? How can they do this?"

It was an instinctive reaction. I was looking for a place to direct my anger. It's not a reaction I'm proud of, but there is no escaping that that's what I felt in those few brief moments. The difference between my dejection then, and the rush of what would have been one of the greatest moments in our sports history, was *one-tenth of a mark*. I had actually won four judges outright; Brian had won three. The Danish and the Swiss judges each had us tied, but they gave Brian an extra point for technical merit. Brian rose to the occasion. He had a technically excellent program, but had either the Swiss or Dane given me an extra tenth for artistic merit, I would have been Olympic champion. Worse, had the Japanese judge joined with the other eight, and placed me first in artistic marks, I would have won. That really stung.

All these realizations were thrust upon me in a matter of seconds as I sat in the "kiss 'n cry" waiting area at rinkside, the television cameras pointed at me. David Santee was the interviewer for ABC-TV and he moved in beside me to get my remarks. He said something like, "There's good news and bad news, Brian. The good news, those are good artistic marks, and the bad — you're second," and he stuck the microphone in my face. It was a difficult time for him, too, and he just didn't carry it off. Apparently the switchboard at the Calgary CTV station lit up with complaints and a couple of days later I got a telegram from ABC-TV apologizing for the incident. Actually, his remark didn't affect me as much as it affected the people in the audience. I'd known for a few seconds that I'd lost. I struggled through the interview as best as I could, because I just wanted to get out of there. My disappointment was oppressing.

As I left the interview area, I was drained and in a state of shock. I still couldn't believe that four years had been reduced to this. I went past Debbie Wilkes and asked her how close it was, and that's when I found out it was 5-4. I asked her if I had the Canadian judge, Jean Matthews, and she said I did, which was something.

I walked under the stands, and the first person I saw was Linda Leaver, Brian's coach. We shook hands and I congratulated her. Sandra Bezic, his choreographer, gave me a hug and said she was sorry. Then I saw Denise Benning, and for the first time, I couldn't contain my disappointment. I broke into tears. Of course, the cameras were catching all of this, so I tried to recompose myself, and then went into the dressing room.

There was Brian Boitano. He looked at me with real concern and said, "What can I say?" Then he turned to Peter Jensen and said softly, "This has been so, so hard." I was grateful to Brian and I respect him for the way he handled himself. He probably just wanted to scream for joy, but he didn't. He knew how I felt — he had been there the year before. He said in interviews later that I hadn't gloated the year before, and he wasn't going to gloat now. Still, it must have been very difficult for him.

Peter walked into the washroom and I sat down on the bench, and feeling comfortable with him, I just sobbed. By now my bitterness toward the judges had dissipated. I kept saying between sobs, "It was so close, it was so close." He didn't say anything. What could he say? I was trying to be as quiet as I could, because I didn't want Brian to hear me. I didn't want it to be hard on him. He shouldn't have to feel bad that he won.

Teresa Moore came in and said gingerly, "I guess I'm the last person that you want to see right now," and we laughed, and I said, "Well let's go out and get it over with," meaning the press. I didn't even have time to devise any kind of strategy for dealing with what would be coming up. On the way to the press interviews, I suffered another sudden attack of emotion. With the cameras following us, I grabbed Teresa and we went off into a corner and I moaned, "I can't do this!" and started to cry again. It was just so difficult to come to grips with what had happened in the last quarter-hour. I kept thinking back to 1984. Teresa is a wonderfully patient person: she waited and helped as I took a few deep breaths to get myself back together again. We went off, and I was fine. Each interview was timed just right. The television people went really easy with me, and just as I felt myself get choked up again, it would be time for the interview to end.

I was feeling together again, and was beginning to develop some perspective, when they announced it was time to go back out for the medals. I knew it was going to be tough. The last time I had stepped onto the ice, I felt I was going to be coming off as Olympic champion: now I was going back on as the runner-up. I had gone into the Olympics wanting all or nothing. I had never thought about how I would handle second place. And I wasn't sure how the audience was going to take it.

They announced Brian as the winner and he skated out to a huge ovation. As they began to announce the silver-medallist, Brian Orser, the roof fell in. It was like thunder. I started to cry again, because the audience had made things better. They were saying, "It's okay, Brian, to be second. We still like you." It was very warming. For the first time, I began to feel a little settled about the situation.

I got on the podium and Brian gave me a big hug and the crowd went nuts again. That surge of emotion from the crowd was, I think, a recognition of what they had just witnessed. People left the building emotionally drained, and talking about what a great event they had all been a part of. After the medal presentations and "The Star-Spangled Banner," I saw my parents for the first time. They were in the stands, at the edge of the boards. They both hugged me. My mother was crying and my dad told me they loved me and were very proud of me.

There were a lot of things to do, which was good, because it gave me some focus. The main chore was going through dope control, a good place to relax, collect your thoughts and have a couple of beers. The beers help to restore a sense of humor, which is a necessity for facing the main press conference. The press conference was difficult. We were all up there: Doug, Brian, myself, Linda Leaver and Sandra Bezic. But, again, they were gentle on us, and I appreciated that. I tried to answer the tough questions as well as I could.

I guess the only irritation in the whole press thing over the next few days was Sandra Bezic. I was very disappointed in her. She was going on to the press that people are now saying about Boitano "he was wonderful," and about Orser they'll be saying "he was wonderful but . . . ." She questioned whether my music and program were appropriate to my style. Who was she to say that I picked the wrong kind of music and program, especially when I got higher marks artistically than her program did?

Brian had been so great about it. People were asking him why he wasn't gloating. He answered, "Because one of my best friends feels so poorly." Sandra turned a lot of that feeling sour, and a lot of people commented on it.

I went to a party afterward — it was supposed to be a victory celebration — at the Coca-Cola hospitality building on the grounds, but the party was very flat. They had a big bottle of champagne for me. They all cheered and sang "O Canada" when I came in. There were some speeches, but everyone was hurting for me. And I was feeling bad.

After another small party at Canada House, my family went back to their accommodation in Canmore, and I went back to the athletes' village at about 4:00 A.M.

I knew when I came into the village that I'd face some people who didn't know what to say. The security people, some athletes who had finished their events, were all supportive. It would be like that for a couple of days. It was uncomfortable for me because I knew it was uncomfortable for other people.

I opened the door to the room I had arranged for, and saw one lonely bed. I had a very weird, painful feeling. It was far from the optimism of a few hours ago when I thought I'd be returning as Canada's first men's Olympic champion. I thought I would cry myself to sleep in my loneliness, but I forced myself not to. I lay down and closed my eyes, but I kept saying to myself, "I can't believe this has happened. I just can't believe this has happened." I couldn't think of anything else. After about an hour I finally dropped off. I had to be up at 7:00 A.M. for a full day of interviews, but I kept waking up every few minutes as if it was all a bad dream.

After a tiring day of interviews, reliving the events of the worst night of my life, they held the nightly medal ceremony in Olympic Plaza downtown. We'd had our official medals the night before, but they wanted to recognize us in the Plaza, along with the other medal-winners of the weekend. During the other presentations, before I even went out, the 40,000 people there started chanting, "OR-SER, OR-SER." I got a tremendous rush. Brian Boitano turned to me and just said, "Wow." They cheered for Brian when he went out, and when I came out they went bananas. It was overwhelming. Because I am harder on myself than anyone else, I had expected it to be different — cooler, I guess. The Plaza crowd was telling me it was okay to come second. I felt embraced by Canadians.

I also took part in the CBC-Radio comedy program, "The Royal Canadian Air Farce." I was in a skit with Big Bobby and Big Jim, and it had a lot of good lines in it: "Hey man, like, nice pin around your neck. Wanta trade it for a Hidi and Howdi pin?" The live audience hadn't expected me. They thought it would be another gag, but when I came out, they stood up and applauded. It was another message to me from Canadians and I continued to thank them. When it came down to the end, when I needed *them*, they were there for me.

I came out of Calgary with a pretty good feeling, ready to tackle the final month of my amateur career. Admittedly, every once in a while I would suffer a major attack of disappointment. I had wanted so much to become Canada's first male Olympic gold-medallist, and I guess I didn't know how mammoth a wish it was until it wasn't fulfilled. As I waited for the my eighth and final World championship, I felt very relaxed and I didn't know if that was good or bad. I did recognize how different it seemed from any time in the previous year. That was another realization: I hadn't understood how much pressure there was until it, too, had gone.

Canadian fans had been good to me in Calgary. When I went through my mail when I got home, I found that it was all really positive. A lot of the letters dealt directly with a column in the *Toronto Star* that had criticized me mercilessly for not doing the second triple axel. The writer suggested that even Eddie Shack could do a double axel and, basically, called me a loser.

The column bothered me a lot. No one wants to be called a loser. When you've made a major contribution to figure skating, as I feel I have, there is no way that I'm a loser. Even though I didn't become Olympic champion, I still feel that I came out a winner.

I was anxious to get to Budapest. I was spending a lot of

time at the Cricket Club, working on my own. At the Olympics I was starting to feel a little claustrophobic, because there were so many people around me. I just needed some space of my own. Doug came down from Orillia a couple of times to work with me, and I also spent some time with him in Barrie.

When I stepped off the ice after my final practice in Barrie, I felt a wave of nostalgia sweep over me. I had been skating on that ice for seventeen years and now it was over. I had had an even more moving experience at the Brian Orser Arena in Orillia just before leaving for the Olympics. I didn't know if I would ever skate there again. It was likely that between Olympics and Worlds I wouldn't have much time in Orillia, and Doug had finally given up on the city and was moving his operation to Barrie. So I took a long look around that rink. I looked at the music room, and thought back with nostalgia to all the programs that had been pumped out of there. I saw the big heaters that Doug and all the skaters had worked so hard to pay for. And there, on the south wall, was the big, big sign that boasted: "You're in Triple Axel Country," and underneath it a list of the accomplishments of Doug's skaters — Michelle, Robert Tebby, myself, Matthew Hall and others. That last day, I searched the walls, hoping to find a patch that had survived fifteen years of repainting, but couldn't. I had been one of the first people to step on the ice at that rink, and now I was leaving it. It was impossible not to experience flashbacks to all the exhilarating, happy, warm, tearful, frightening and painful moments on that frozen 15,000 square feet where I had spent so much of my life.

In between Olympics and Worlds, I also made the big break with the north. I finally left the small town and moved to Toronto. Since I would be turning professional after Budapest, and would be travelling frequently, I needed to be near the airport. I also had the restaurant business in Toronto. Tim Grech, my close friend and business partner, and I had expanded our operations to a second location and will eventually have three or four more sites. I had also become national spokesman for NutraSweet. It simply became necessary to take up residence in Toronto, so I leased an apartment in Willowdale, close to the airport and the restaurants.

I had mixed feelings during the interval before Worlds. I did spend some time stewing about the 1984 Olympics, but most of my thoughts were positive. Then, on the final day of training, I had a bad practice. I was really down, then. I didn't want to go. I felt that I wasn't ready. I wondered why they held Worlds in an Olympic year. There were all these kinds of irrational doubts. But I got on the plane and flew to Budapest.

I began reading a book called *Handbook to a Higher Consciousness* by Kenneth Keyes. It was an interesting study, and helped me to put things into perspective. The main theme was to take and enjoy each moment as it comes. And that's how I started feeling for Worlds. It was my last Worlds; I was going to enjoy it, savor the friendships and not carry any burdens through it. I went to a lot of practices. I watched friends like Rob and Tracy go through their routines, and I collected and stored away memories. I just took it all in and enjoyed every moment.

It took a while to work myself into this state of mind. I had some help, particularly from Tracy and Rob. It was fortunate that I took that approach, considering what happened during the figures judging.

The figures were the same set as those required at the Olympics. I went out to choose my ice for the first figure, the right outside rocker. As I picked my ice the referee — who oversees the nine-person judging panel — came up to speak to me. It was Ben Wright of the u.s., and I knew that I might have trouble when I saw that he was on the panel. He apologized, saying that the ice wasn't very good and that it was really hard to see. This was totally uncalled for. He wasn't warning me: it was more of a psyche-out. The *last* thing you need to hear before you push off is, "It's really hard to see." A nice piece of work.

I chuckled to myself about the absurdity of it, reselected my ice, went through my whole mental routine again, and did a pretty good figure. They marked me fifth on it. That shocked me, because it was just as good as, or better than, the Olympic figure. Then it was the double-three. It was good and bad. It was traced nicely and had a good center, but the side line-up was off. I gave them something to mark me down on, so I can't say anything about being fifth again in that figure. My loop was the best ever. It was much better than the one I did in Cincinnati when I won the figure, but somehow, I was still only fourth in that one, and fifth over all. I saw some of the other guys' loops and they were unbelievable — Doug was beside himself with anger. Fadeev's loop was right off axis; it wasn't traced that well; and he won it. Boitano's was off axis; the loops themselves were big; and he was third.

Fadeev won the figures, Boitano was third, Fischer fourth and Grzegorz Filipowski of Poland slipped into second, which actually saved me. Had Brian been second and me fifth, the competition would have been over right then. As it was, I still had to win the short and long to win the gold.

Right after the event, I was talking to the Canadian judge, Jean Matthews and she was upset. Even though there was another hour of ice time, the panel had been rushed by the referee, Ben Wright. He pushed them. The judges were given very little time to look at the figures, and very little time to find the mark. They just had to go by instinct, or what they knew of the placing so far.

Now, judges aren't supposed to know what the standings are in any one figure. The thinking is that, if they did, they would mark according to that placing, not what they saw with their eyes. A judge who had a skater low might move him up, and vice-versa. At the end of each figure, the judges are locked into a room until it's time for the next one. Of course, there are little hand signs that go back and forth from the spectators to a judge. A federation member might hold up a finger to let a judge know where the skater from his country is standing, but there is really no way of letting him in on the complete order.

This time though, after the first figure, Ben Wright apparently came in and put the results of the figure — which had me fifth and Brian second — on the table in the judges' room. He said that he didn't think he was supposed to do that — in fact, it's plainly against the rules — but now that everyone had seen them, anyway, he just left them there. It might have affected the way some judges judged the event.

The short program was the next day and about an hour before it was to start, Grzegorz Filipowski came up to me and said, "It's so different when you're seventh and eighth [as he had been for several years] and just fighting to move up. And it's so nerve-wracking being in the medals and trying to stay there. I can't believe that you guys have been doing this for so many years." It was kind of nice to hear an acknowledgement of the pressure the top skaters endure.

Grzegorz had trouble in the short program, missing his combination, but he wasn't alone. There weren't many clean ones. Chris Bowman of the United States missed his combination and another American, Paul Wylie, botched his spin. The only ones who skated cleanly were Petr Barna of Czechoslovakia, Heiko Fischer and Brian Boitano.

Boitano skated first in the final group of the short (and the long) and I was scheduled to be fourth. I wasn't really that nervous, although I was suddenly thrown off my normal timing. Fadeev was supposed to perform one skater before me, but he had injured his groin again on a double axel in warm-up. Just before he was to take to the ice, he withdrew, which meant that I had to skate sooner than I had expected. I didn't do my normal walkthrough. I had to hurry it, and then take to the ice. My first double axel, which is normally an indicator of how I will do, was excellent, so I thought, "Fine, I'm having a good program." Maybe it was over-confidence, but when I went into the triple-axel combination I came down and wasn't over my skates. I stumbled out of it, put my hand down and couldn't do the double loop to follow. The rest of the program was fine, but it was a full 0.6 deduction. My technical marks were all 5.3-5.4 and only my artistic — 5.9s — saved me. I knew the gold was gone, because Brian had skated well. But since Victor Petrenko, Kotin and a lot of others had missed their combinations (maybe because people were flat after the Olympics) I still finished second in the short. I thought I would be fifth or sixth, but the second wasn't a gift: everyone else did poorly, too.

To win the gold, I would have to win the long, and someone else would have to beat Boitano. This wasn't going to happen, because he was too consistent. But I wasn't depressed, I just wanted to go out and skate my final long program as well as I could. My friends gave me a lot of help with that, filled me full of positive thoughts, and I used the book to point me in that direction.

Kurt Browning, twice silver-medallist at Canadians, was skating first in the second-last group and was going to try the quadruple toe loop, which had never been landed. Both he and Brian had tried one the year before and missed. I stood near the monitor to watch Kurt. About twenty feet away Brian Boitano was warming up with his coach, Linda Leaver. Brian was also going to be trying a quad when our group had its turn. Kurt's music started. His first jump was the quad and he landed it. The whole arena went completely crazy. You could feel the thunder down where we were. Linda went over and asked a u.s. official if he had done it and the official said yes. Linda walked back to tell Brian that Kurt had done it — but he had no visible reaction. I knew that he wanted to be the first to do it, and I think that might have thrown him off in his long program. He missed his quad, and didn't do any triple axels — the quad takes the place of one, and the second one was singled. It wasn't a superb program by any means, but enough to finish second, which is all he needed.

I was very happy for Kurt. He works hard and it's great to see a Canadian making a splash like that on the world scene. He did a little turn after the quad, as Vern Taylor did after his triple axel, but I knew it was going to count. In landing the quad, he also extended a proud Canadian tradition. The last three jumping barriers have all been broken by Canadians: Donald Jackson with the triple Lutz; Vern Taylor with the triple axel; and now Kurt with the quad. It was a marvelous moment. Funny, in a sense I've been there for all three. I was born just before Donald's jump; I was in the audience for Vern's; and ten years later, Kurt's came on my final day as an amateur.

It was a boost to see the quad, although I had to get back into my own space. During the warm-up, I spotted Rob and Tracy in audience. The night before, they had skated a wonderful freedance and they knew how important it was to me to finish with a great performance. I was pumped up for it, although I knew I couldn't win the gold.

I was really nervous, and scared at the same time. I wanted to skate well. I was afraid of falling. I was thinking about my future and knew that I had to skate well for that, and to satisfy my own expectations.

I saw Scott Hamilton just before I went out. He had been feeling bad for me because of the Olympics, and he gave me a warm, knowing nod, sending over some positive vibes.

There was the normal conference with Doug, Uschi and Peter before the announcer called my name. Nothing unusual or overly significant was said, although it was to be my last four and a half minutes as an amateur.

Then I went out and gave the performance of my life.

The first triple axel, in combination with the double toe, came off well. Then, soon after that, I landed the triple flip and knew that I was fine. I breathed a sigh of relief because that was the last triple flip I would ever do in my life — it's pulled right out of my professional repertoire. I did double out a triple, but that was planned. I'd been having trouble with the loop in practice all week, and I knew that I was going to try the second triple axel. Everything was precise, the program just flew and it was loaded with emotion. It was far better than the Olympics, although I had been happy with the Olympic program. I headed into the second triple axel and it was amazing. I think it was even better than the first one.

I took my usual bow, but nothing really hit me until I sat down in the "kiss 'n cry" area. Doug and Peter were all lit up. Uschi, of course, was crying. I realized that in my farewell statement, I had given the very best skate of my career, including all those good short programs. I had been in a daze but the three of them, so pleased for me because it was my final routine, shocked me into understanding that I had skated outstandingly. Brian Boitano, Linda Leaver and Sandra Bezic were right there, too, and they all gave me warm hugs of congratulations. They were the first ones to come up to me. That meant a lot. Through all of this, Brian and I managed to maintain our strong friendship. At the end of the competition one writer, speaking on behalf of all the press, thanked both of us for being so good with them while we were both under so much pressure in the past couple of years.

I easily won the long program, although two judges — the Austrian and Polish — had me second, which was absurd. Since no one else beat Brian Boitano, he won his second gold of the year and third in three years, but I wasn't sad at all. I was relieved, and just happy I'd skated well.

Then the marks came up: in the second set there were three perfect 6.0s, including one from the Russian judge. That really set the crowd off and gave me another chill. In my era, there had only been four perfect marks given out in men's skating. They were all given this year, and all for my long programs. Just to make things complete, after the judging was over, Ben Wright told the panel that the 6.0s were uncalled for, although he did concede that the Canadian judge could be excused for her 6.0. Perfect.

So I won my fourth World silver medal, and sixth including the two Olympics. My plans did not include that final ISU tour through Europe, because I really needed a break, although I did intend to skate with Tommy Collins's North American ISU tour. That would be my market when I was a pro.

It was then that the ISU played some hardball. Earlier that day, Rob and Tracy had gone to the ISU and had been told that if they didn't do the European tour, they wouldn't be allowed to do Tommy's tour. I knew before my long program that I would have to deal with the ISU and wasn't looking forward to it. I was determine to go home after the Sunday exhibitions. My dad had talked to David Dore and Bob Howard of the CFSA, suggesting they accompany me to the meeting. They did come along, and so did Tracy and Rob. David said we all had things to do at home. There was a big change in our careers coming up, and we needed the time. The ISU said to take the time during Tommy's tour, and then Beat Hasler of the ISU said that if we didn't skate, the union would pull the World championships from Halifax in 1990. I was proud of David because he shot back, "Fine. Pull it. These kids can't do the tour." Finally Hasler agreed that we could do part of the tour. We Canadians had a meeting and decided we'd stay in Budapest and accompany the others for the first two weeks of the tour, leaving after the London stop, halfway through the itinerary.

We kind of broke the ground for everyone. Liz Manley would come in with Brian Boitano, halfway through at London, to replace us.

Doug left Budapest on the Sunday, but there was really no special moment for us. He keeps a lot of things inside and, as I've mentioned before, there are so many feelings which pass between us without words. He doesn't get emotional and although I get emotional with other people, it was never that way with Doug. But all week I sat back and watched him and realized how far *he* had come too, how much he had grown. Like me, he was a small-town boy who had climbed the top of the world. He had learned it all on his own — or rather, we learned it together. I was proud of him and of us. For seventeen years, almost to the day, he had been my coach. And despite all the others who'd helped, he was *the* coach. There had never been any doubt about that. And now our coach-skater relationship had drawn to a close as I joined the professional ranks. We handled it as we had the previous seventeen years — professionally.

With Uschi it was different. Our special moment came during the exhibitions on Sunday. I skated a routine to "The Story of My Life," and when I came off she was sobbing. I changed costumes to the outfit from the 1986 short program — the Hungarian folkdance — and the Budapest crowd went crazy. They were still cheering as I came off the ice and hugged Uschi. Then we pulled back and just looked at each other. For us that spoke volumes: thank-you, congratulations, it-was-wonderful, what-can-I-say?

Uschi left for home the next day and I stayed on for my required two-week stint with the tour. Suddenly, the snowball had stopped rolling and I was reflecting back on everything: all the other tours; my relationship with my friends on the tour; all the great moments; all the down moments. Each year on tour, I had taken time to reflect on the season that had passed. On this final go-round, I was casting my mind back not just on 1988 but also through eight years of world competition. I never enjoyed the events more than when I looked back on them during that two weeks in late March and early April, 1988. It was a neat feeling, but no one had ever warned me it would happen. I think a lot of us were experiencing the same sense of impending loss. We couldn't get close enough to each other. We couldn't share enough stories. The Big Chill, twenty years in advance.

Katarina and I spent a lot of time talking on that tour. When the tour stopped in Karl-Marxstadt in East Germany, Katarina invited Tracy and Rob, Bestemianova and Bukin, Valova and Vassiliev and myself — all the old regulars — over to her apartment for champagne. She toasted us all and said, "I hope that we can all stay this close in the future." It was touching. Natalia and Andrei were skating together for the last time. In retirement, they would split up, because she would join her husband in his Soviet touring company. I guess Igor Bobrin finally has a partner for that pairs routine.

It wasn't all old friends though. I had started with a group that included the likes of David Santee and Scott Hamilton, all long since turned pro, but on this tour there were some of the stars of the future. Kurt Browning, who won a freeskating bronze medal, giving Canada two of the three medals in freestyle in 1988, I think for the first time ever, was along and I couldn't help feeling that I was looking at myself in a mirror from eight years previously. He asked me a lot of questions; I gave him some advice. He was arriving at a critical point, where it would no longer be enough for him just to skate well and hope to place highly. He is on the verge of being in the medals, and will be if his figures improve .... Sound familiar?

Kurt took a quantum leap in 1988. He made an indelible impact with the quadruple jump, just as I had with the triple axel in my first year. He has arrived. He has a lot to learn, some growing to do, but that's fine because he has time on his side. Someone asked me if I thought he was a worthy heir to the Canadian title, and I answered "yes" immediately. I think it's in capable hands.

My competitive career had ended the moment I stepped off the ice in Budapest. The ensuing two weeks were time for nostalgia, self-examination and sharing of memories. But when the tour stopped in London it was time for me to say some goodbyes and head home.

On Tom's tour, I would be a full-fledged professional. When that transatlantic flight ended and the plane touched down at Pearson International Airport, I had cast off the only lifestyle I had known for nearly twenty years: early-morning figures practices, competitive tension and being at the mercy of a judging panel. I stepped off the plane and into a new phase of my life.

Epilogue

Figure skating offers an opportunity that is rare in the world of big-time sport: the best-known athletes are amateur; yet competitors leaving amateur ranks can continue to make a good living from the sport for much of the rest of their lives.

The most successful and charismatic of the amateurs can command huge fees as headliners in one of the touring professional ice shows. Alternatively, they can start their own shows, as Torvill and Dean did. After their initial impact on the public has worn off, they can extend their professional skating careers by accepting less-prominent billing in the same shows. There are also a few professional competitions, including the World Professional Championships in Landover, Maryland, which are becoming increasingly popular among both skaters and television audiences. The winner can take home as much as $50,000.

Coaching is another avenue open to retiring amateur skaters. Big names can command well over $30 an hour. However, few stars begin coaching until after they have performed profes-

sionally. Brian Orser feels that if he coaches, it will be well in the future, and that it will never be a full-time occupation. He has his expanding restaurant business, and prefers the performance aspect of skating to teaching.

A professional's status as a headliner can last anywhere from one to twenty years. The average time at the top is four years, because every fourth year there is another batch of retiring Olympic stars ready to trade on their success.

A big name can command $1,000,000 a year from a top show. Scott Hamilton was still making well over $1,000,000 five years after he had retired from competition. Toller Cranston, Dorothy Hamill and Peggy Fleming also managed to maintain their star status long after the peers of their amateur years had faded away.

It is estimated that Brian Boitano, as Olympic champion, will earn $1.75 million in his first professional season. Brian Orser's potential income was probably sliced in half by that one-tenth of a point difference between gold and silver in Calgary, yet he will probably gross about $750,000 in his first professional season.

But it is not the money — Orser has never complained about the lost income — that will keep the eight-time Canadian champion in front of an audience. He simply loves to express himself on the ice. He will probably continue to perform for six to eight years as a professional. It will be in the first two or three years, however, when his market value is highest, that Orser will skate the most.

The life of a professional is in some ways more gruelling than that of an amateur. During his seventeen-year amateur career, Orser trained eleven months a year. Most of his days began at dawn. From 1979 to 1981, he was on the ice for ten to twelve hours a day. After that, refining his training techniques, he cut his workload down to between six and eight hours a day. Over his amateur career, he spent some 20,000 hours in training. That's more than two full years — twenty-four hours a day — with skates on.

A professional skater doesn't spend nearly as much time train-

ing. In fact, Orser found that he had to begin working out in a gym, "because my body kept screaming at me, that it was getting stiff."

Orser expects to live out of a suitcase for six months each year, when he's on the road with Stars on Ice and a fledgling Canadian tour organized by the CFSA. The travelling is wearying. Moreover, a professional skater has to find a different kind of motivation to perform well. The excitement and intense pressure of competition is motivation enough to inspire an amateur, but show professionals depend upon their audience. The crowd reaction, not medals, is the indication of how well they're doing. That's why professional skaters can often be seen peeking out at the audience — checking its size and mood — before their turn to skate.

Constantly on the move, and without a home rink, professionals may train for only an hour a day. Of course, they don't have four hours of figures practice to worry about.

The headliners have to deliver about fifteen minutes of physically tiring and emotionally draining skating each night. The top skaters usually perform two separate numbers and a pair of encores in every show.

In a touring company, professional skaters can become close friends, but the relationships among them are not as intense as those that develop on an ISU tour. Professionals are of varying ages. They have matured and kindled more outside interests. Amateurs on an ISU tour tend to be younger, and have just endured together a year of gruelling competition.

And professional tours seem to be far less international in flavor — although there are exceptions. For their appeal to distinct markets, Europeans tend to tour Europe, while North Americans tour North America.

On our last European tour, the Soviet Olympic pairs champion, Sergei Grinkov, was talking about how tired he had become. The older skaters were amazed because he was only twenty-one. But I began thinking how he must feel, knowing that he has to go back to Moscow and prepare new programs, spending eight hours a day for nine months honing his skills for six and a half minutes at the World championship.

It made me realize that I had made the right decision in turning professional. My amateur career had been a fascinating ride, but I was ready to climb off. I will probably skate in a CFSA Canadian show tour and then join my old friend and rival Scott Hamilton in Stars on Ice, which runs through thirty cities in the United States (but not in consecutive weeks.) I'll still have time to come home and work with the restaurant business.

Since 1986, I had considered myself a skating "veteran." At my final Worlds and on tour, I took a lot of time to enjoy what was happening and to reflect upon my years in competitive sport.

I feel great about my career, proud of what I accomplished. If I had won the Olympics, it would have been gravy. What is most important is that I've grown as a man, even more than I've advanced as a skater. That's the result of all the travelling and international contact, and because I came second so many times, and had to deal with coming second in the Olympics. I'm sure there will be huge disappointments in the future that will seem easier to handle because of that.

I think a lot of people never thought there would be a second golden era of Canadian figure skating. I was proud to be a leader of that. So much of the revival has to be attributed to David Dore, who gave all of us a goal.

I was very happy for Liz Manley, who rose to great heights to win silver medals in her final two performances. It really was a superb finish for our group which had been together for so long. Rob and Tracy and I were talking on tour about our era, and we realized that most of us became really motivated when Karen Magnussen won her gold medal in 1973. In my case, there was Karen's win combined with Donald Jackson coming to my club a little earlier. That led us to think that fifteen years after the Calgary Olympics, we should have the same kind of spectacular skating team again. There are all kinds of outstanding athletes in Canada, but we'll never see them at the World level if they aren't inspired to take up figure skating. Apparently, during and after the Olympics, skating registration in Canada — and, I assume, the United States — took a sharp upswing. This will show some positive results for us in the future.

How will skating history judge me? Well, I know I don't want to be remembered as the guy who always finished second. But I think nights like those in Calgary will help me to retain a long-term reputation as a great skater. I admit I always wanted to be remembered on my own, as my own little legend in skating. Although Brian Boitano skated brilliantly at the Olympics, I don't think he took away my limelight; I think he joined it. Skating fans, who are quite knowledgeable, tend to look back on all the years in an athlete's career.

It was too bad I didn't win the Olympics, but it was a brilliant night of skating regardless, and people will always remember us as The Two Brians. My World championship was very important, of course. And so was the farewell performance in Budapest, because people will recognize that long program for what it was. It had its own pressure after the Olympic results. As my personal curtain call, it was probably the best men's singles performance by anyone in the years I was involved. I think I'll probably be remembered more as an artistic skater, and that's ironic, because people said I would always be deficient in that area. Yet, in that final program of my career, I received three perfect marks for artistic impression.

I don't want to champion myself too much, but I feel that I set trends throughout my career. When I was consistently landing triple axels so long ago, everyone scrambled to get an axel into the program. As they did that, I was already moving into the artistic side, then the shift started to go that way. I feel I welded them together in the final two years. The overriding fear in the early 1980s was that the sport was becoming overly technical and I think I moved its direction off that track a little. Even Brian Boitano, a superb technical skater, followed that trend in 1988.

It might be that, with respect to figures, I was an era too early. But I learned a lot from figures that helped me in freeskating. I labored so hard to bring them up to third best in the world that I don't regret it. I'm proud of that improvement.

Peering back to those early days in Midland and Penetang, it always shocks me how far I've come. Not so much in public recognition, because anyone can get public recognition. I'm more stunned at what I've done, at being the best in the world at something. Every once in a while, I say to myself ". . . in the *entire world*." Even if no one ever recognized or applauded me, I'd still feel the same burst of pleasure over that. To bring recognition to Canada at the same time only made it sweeter.

And finally, it's not the awards or trophies or parades that have meant the most to me, but the people. I think that's a positive outgrowth of the family I grew up in. Long, long after skating is over, I'll still cherish the friendships I've forged through skating.

The only excessively emotional time came for me on that final ISU tour which, in retrospect, I'm glad I participated in. Katarina, Natalia, Andrei, Tracy, Rob, myself and a few others were all in a room, talking about our lives, our families and our homelands. There were Canadians, Russians, East Germans, Americans.

It may be a cliché, and it happens in other disciplines when performers from East and West get together, but there was absolutely no sense of politics or nationalism. It was hard for us to imagine that there were any barriers between us. We were warmed by the same feelings, had shared such similar competitive experiences and we were all going to miss one another. We yearned for it to go on forever.

People talk about world peace and I wish that there was some way to extend the experiences of international athletes to everyone. Thus enlightened, we would have a much greater chance of achieving that world peace.

It is for extending me the opportunity to reach that under-standing that I am most grateful to sport.

Appendix

BRIAN ORSER'S COMPETITIVE RECORD

December 1974	Ontario Games	Thunder Bay, Ont.	First
January 1975	Canada Games	Lethbridge, Alta.	First
January 1977	Canadian Nationals (Novices)	Calgary, Alta.	First
January 1978	Canadian Nationals (Junior)	Victoria, B.C.	Third
March 1978	Junior Worlds	Mégève, France	Fourth
February 1979	Canadian Nationals (Junior)	Thunder Bay, Ont.	First
September 1979	Vienna Cup	Vienna, Austria	Third
January 1980	Canadian Nationals	Kitchener, Ont.	Fourth
August 1980	Grand Prix	St. Gervais, France	First
August 1980	Nebelhorn Trophy	Oberstdorf, W. Germany	Second
October 1980	Skate Canada	Calgary, Alta.	Sixth
January 1981	Canadian Nationals	Halifax, N.S.	First
March 1981	Worlds	Hartford, Conn.	Sixth
September 1981	St. Ivel	Richmond, England	First
October 1981	Skate Canada	Ottawa, Ont.	Second
January 1982	Canadian Nationals	Brandon, Man.	First

March 1982	Worlds	Copenhagen, Denmark	Fourth
September 1982	St. Ivel	Richmond, England	First
October 1982	Skate Canada	Kitchener, Ont.	Second
February 1983	Canadian Nationals	Montreal, Quebec	First
March 1983	Worlds	Helsinki, Finland	Third
October 1983	Skate Canada	Halifax, N.S.	First
November 1983	Ennia Cup	The Hague, Netherlands	First
January 1984	Canadian Nationals	Regina, Sask.	First
February 1984	Winter Olympics	Sarajevo, Yugoslavia	Second
March 1984	Worlds	Ottawa, Ont.	Second
October 1984	Skate Canada	Victoria, B.C.	First
November 1984	NHK	Tokyo, Japan	Second
February 1985	Canadian Nationals	Moncton, N.B.	First
March 1985	Worlds	Tokyo, Japan	Second
September 1985	St. Ivel	Richmond, England	First
November 1985	NHK	Kobe, Japan	Second
February 1986	Canadian Nationals	North Bay, Ont.	First
March 1986	Worlds	Geneva, Switzerland	Second
November 1986	Novarat International	Budapest, Hungary	First
January 1987	Canadian Nationals	Ottawa, Ont.	First
March 1987	Worlds	Cincinnati, Ohio	First
October 1987	Skate Canada	Calgary, Alta.	First
January 1988	Canadian Nationals	Victoria, B.C.	First
February 1988	Winter Olympics	Calgary, Alta.	Second
March 1988	Worlds	Budapest, Hungary	Second